React from Zero

Learn React with the JavaScript you already know

Kay Plößer

FULLSTACK.*io*

React from Zero

Learn React with the JavaScript you already know

Written by Kay Plößer
Edited by Nate Murray

Cover Art by TJ Fuller.
Published by Fullstack.io.

Questions? Email us at: us@fullstack.io

Sample code download available at:
fullstackreact.com/react-from-zero/code

Contents

Book Revision

Revision 3p for print - 2019-02-28

Bug Reports

If you'd like to report any bugs, typos, or suggestions just email us at: **react@fullstack.io**.

Be notified of updates via Twitter

If you'd like to be notified of updates to the book on Twitter, follow us at @full-stackio[1].

We'd love to hear from you!

Did you like the book? Did you find it helpful? We'd love to add your face to our list of testimonials on the website! Email us at: react@fullstack.io.

---

[1]https://twitter.com/fullstackio

FULLSTACK.io

Download the
Example Code

This book contains several example apps and code samples.
Because you purchased the paperback version you can
download this code for free at our website.

URL https://fullstackreact.com/react-from-zero/code/

BOOK
SERIAL AMZ-RFZ4HZ·
CODE

Learn more at: fullstackreact.com/react-from-zero/code/

To download the code, visit the URL above and enter your
email and serial code and we'll email you the code.

How This Book Is Structured

React From Zero is split into two parts, each with multiple chapters. Every chapter tries to teach a single feature of React by presenting code examples and explaining them in detail.

The goal if this book is to demystify React and connect it to "everyday" JavaScript. Unlike many tutorials which use React as a "black box", we're going to start from the bottom and work our way up.

Part I: Basics

Part I of this book is about the **basic usage of React**.

We learn how React works by starting with **JavaScript you already know**.

First we setup a development environment and then we start by digging into the basic JavaScript objects that React components are made of. We'll talk about *why* we use JSX tags when we write React, how to create re-usable *components* and how we can next them to make more complex structures.

In **Part I** we'll teach you the skills that you'll use in 80% of your day-to-day work with React.

Part II: Additions

Part II of this book is about the **advanced features of React**.

We learn about things like refactoring, lifecycle methods, library integration and unit-testing.

Is this book right for me?

We assume that you:

- Have a basic grasp of HTML
- Have a working knowledge of basic JavaScript

I'd guess that you've probably gone through a React tutorial or two before buying this book, but that isn't a requirement.

You **don't** have to be a JavaScript expert and you certainly don't need any existing expertise in React.

We believe this book will be helpful if you've felt like learning React is daunting and you want to understand the core parts in isolation. If you're the type of person who learns by taking things apart and then putting them back together, then I think you'll really like this book.

Getting Started

This book comes with a folder of example code. The code examples load in your browser **without any extra tooling**. You can simply open the .html files in your browser and they should run.

Most of the code blocks in the book will show the name of the file in which you can find that code, like this:

react-from-zero/00-object-elements.html

```
var anotherElement = {
  $$typeof: magicValue,
  ref: null,
  type: "p",
  props: {
    children: "A nice text paragraph."
  }
};
```

As you can see in the heading of that block, the full code for this example can be found in `react-from-zero/00-object-elements.html`.

If you get lost at any point reading the book, open up the code example and look at the code to see the whole context.

Get Excited!

This book is designed to be an easy step-by-step tutorial on learning the basics of React. Don't be intimidated by all of the different pieces in React that you've read about on the web.

Over the next lessons, we're going to walk through the basics of React. By the end, you're going to have a firm foundation on which you can learn to build bigger apps.

Without further ado, let's get started!

– Kay

Part I

The first part of this book is mainly about getting up and running.

We will talk about basic React concepts and learn about 80% of the day-to-day work that we will be facing when building applications with React.

In this part you will learn:

- What a virtual DOM is
- What React elements are and how they are structured
- What JSX is and how it relates to React and JavaScript
- What React components are and how they are structured
- How a whole React application is structured
- How to build a complete application with React

The lessons are rather short, most of them can be done in under 1 hour. Let's dive right into the first chapter!

What's the point of React?

When using a new framework, the first question you should ask is, *"Why should I use it?"* so I want to take a step back and tell you about what makes React a better base for application architecture than, let's say, jQuery.

When we're using React, the problem we're trying to solve is how to update our "HTML" view with **dynamic data** and **user interactions**.

React manages the view layer of your application.

That is, you take your **data** and you pass it to **React** and the output is your "HTML" view.

 I put "HTML" in quotes, because actually what happens is that our browser converts the HTML into *objects* which render the view we see. We call these objects *the DOM*.

At a high level, you can roughly think of what React does as the equation:

```
reactApp(yourData) => rendered view
```

Meaning, we take our React code (which we'll describe below), combine it with our data, and then a new view is rendered in our browser.

So, before we get to React, what are some historic approaches to handling this problem?

jQuery's approach is basically to manipulate the DOM directly. jQuery gives you, as its name implies, *query* methods that allow to get access to DOM elements.

Once you have a reference to a DOM elements you *imperatively* write text into your DOM nodes, add event listeners and so on. The problem with is that this gets unwieldy fast.

It starts small: you add a few elements to a list, change a `<p>` here and there, but as the application grows and requirements change **you end up with hundreds of elements that all need to be updated dynamically**.

If you're not careful the performance of your app can suffer. You're forced to craft some sophisticated algorithms that don't thrash the DOM and bring the browser to its knees.

Furthermore, it's just hard to keep track of the resulting nest of code – it can be difficult to orchestrate those handlers to all work together.

React tries to solve this problem for you and it does it with **the help of a *virtual* DOM** (VDOM), which is just a fancy name for **plain old JavaScript objects** nested to resemble the structure of a DOM.

The idea is, you write your code as if you would simply overwrite/replace your whole DOM.

However, React has some performance optimizations to make this run really fast in reality.

It's a win-win – This approach allows you to focus on your data and UI and frees you from meddling with the details of DOM updates - all while getting super-fast performance.

If you're pretty comfortable with JavaScript, at this point you might be interested in reviewing Appendix A: A Virtual DOM Primer. In that section, we'll walk through the code of building a toy Virtual DOM library.

However, if you're relatively new to JavaScript, you don't need to understand that part just yet.

We'll talk more about the VDOM in a later chapter, but for now, know that the virtual dom **takes a tree of objects** and then **renders a view**.

Again, the **virtual DOM** (VDOM), is just a fancy name for **plain old JavaScript objects** nested to resemble the structure of a DOM.

But **what are the objects that this VDOM requires?** What do they look like?

That's the topic of the next chapter. Let's take a look at the fundamental unit of a React app: **an object element**.

Quiz

1. What are the two problems React tries to solve?
2. What is the main difference between React and jQuery?
3. How does React simplify your code?

Lesson 0 - Object Elements

In order for React to render an object into the DOM, we need to describe *what* we need to be rendered.

Our approach here is going to be a little different than what you've seen in other tutorials: instead of showing you how to use React as a black box, we're going to start at the bottom and work our way up.

We're trying to *demystify* React and connect it to "everyday" JavaScript. To that end, we'll start by creating a **basic JavaScript object** that represents an *element* which React can use to render an element on our screen.

A Simple Element

First I want to show you a simple element object, it only uses the parts that are required by React.

A simple paragraph element implemented as React element would look like this:

react-from-zero/00-object-elements.html

```
var anotherElement = {
  $$typeof: magicValue,
  ref: null,
  type: "p",
  props: {
    children: "A nice text paragraph."
  }
};
```

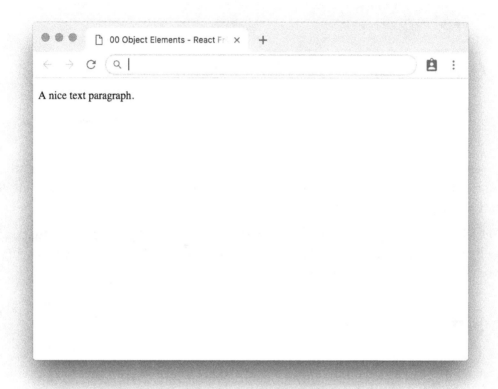

Simple Element

Remember: the idea here is that we are creating a **basic JavaScript object** that will eventually render into an element like this HTML: `<p>A nice text paragraph.</p>`

For this object, the first part `$$typeof` is used by **React** to differentiate between simple objects and React elements.

If it's missing, React will complain. In the example, it uses a variable called `magicValue` which is either the magic number `0xeac7` or `Symbol.for("react.element")`.

`Symbol` is a relatively new object in JavaScript and not all browsers support it. If you use a browser with a JavaScript version that doesn't support symbols, the magic number is used, but if you have an up to date browser, React uses a symbol to mark objects as React elements.

The idea of *symbols* is that they are globally unique. If someone wants to access an attribute that uses a symbol as an object key or tries to check if something equals a specific symbol, they have to explicitly get that symbol with `Symbol.for()` function. With *String* or *Number* equality could happen by accident.

 The term *magic number* can have different meanings in programming. In this case, it means a constant numerical or text value used to identify a file format or protocol. Wikipedia[2]

This magic number is arbitrary. It's just a number selected by the React team as an identifier to be used for all React element objects. You won't need to come up with your own magic numbers when using React, it's just an identifier for the React library.

React creates one of these symbols and then checks if objects contain it inside their `$$typeof` attribute.

The second part of `anotherElement` is the `ref`. It can be used to store a reference to the corresponding DOM element after this React element is rendered into the DOM, but we will talk about this in detail, later in another chapter.

Then we have the `type`. It tells React, what kind of DOM element it should create for this object, in this case, a paragraph. (This maps to the HTML ‹p› tag.)

Finally the `props`. Here you see a `children` prop that is a string. `props` is React's way to **pass data down the element tree**. Discussing this has to wait until another chapter, too.

This element `anotherElement` is the simplest possible React element. It's the "hello world" of React elements, if you will.

We could pass this into the `ReactDOM.render()` function (which we'll talk about in the next chapter) and it would render DOM elements like the HTML:

---

[2]https://en.wikipedia.org/wiki/Magic_number_(programming)

```
<p>A nice text paragraph.</p>
```

Next, let's look at another element, this time with all the optional parts that we left out in this simple example.

A Complex Element

Here's a more complex element that covers additional aspects of the React element API:

react-from-zero/00-object-elements.html

```
var reactElement = {
  // This special property will be checked by React to ensure this
  // object
  // is a React element and not just some user data
  // React.createElement() sets it for you
  $$typeof: magicValue,

  // This will also be checked by React. We will be talking about
  // references later, but if you're not using them, this has to be
  // set to null and not undefined
  ref: null,

  // This defines the HTML-tag
  type: "h1",

  // This defines the properties that get passed down to the element
  props: {
    // In this example there is just a single text node as child
    children: "Hello, world!",

    // a CSS class
    className: "abc",

    // styles can be passed as object literals
```

```
    // React uses camelCase instead of dashed-case (like CSS/D3 do)
    style: {
      textAlign: "center"
    },

    // event handlers can be added as properties, too
    // React uses synthetic events to try to normalize browser
    // behavior
    onClick: function (notYourRegularEvent) {
      alert("click");
    }
  }
};
```

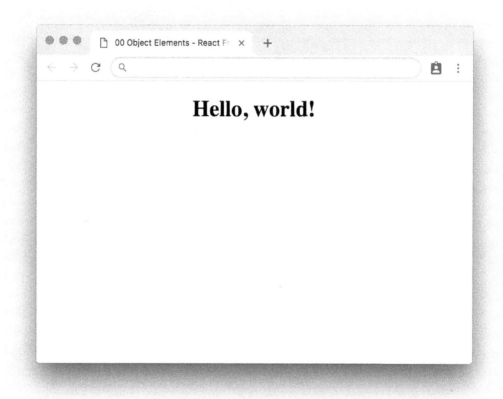

Complex Element

First we have $$typeof, ref, type and props again. Nothing special here, but this time we added props other than children.

There is for example className. It is the React way to add a CSS class attribute to an element, it makes it easy to style your React elements with external CSS.

 The className is a DOM element property used to set the value of class attribute of that element. React avoided using class because it is a reserved word in JavaScript.

Next, there is style. If you write HTML, style is normally a string attribute, but for React it has to be an object. Also, it uses camelCase instead of kebab-case what you would expect from CSS. This allows for simpler transformation of local styles. So in this case, our textAlign key maps to the text-align property in CSS.

At the end, we have onClick. This is the way to add **event handlers** to objects. The difference from HTML is that they are written in camelCase instead of lowercase and you can pass functions directly without the need to wrap them in a string.

Another difference to these handlers is that they get a SyntheticEvent as an argument, rather than a browser's native event. This is done to **normalize events across all browsers** so that events always look the same to our code.

 SyntheticEvents also have a nativeEvent attribute you can use if you need the *real* event for some reason.

 Also, SyntheticEvents are re-used when your function returns, so gather all the data you need from them before you make any asynchronous calls.

Wrap Up

In this lesson, we showed how to define React element with basic objects.

I showed you that **there is no tooling required to get started** and that you can even skip some helper methods and JSX if you want to play around with React.

We also talked about some subtle differences on how React does things that may not match your DOM/HTML experience.

You probably also noticed that using this approach, while being easy to understand the basics, is rather cumbersome for a big project.

While components will provide you with mechanisms to reuse this code, it's still not easy to follow, especially for big elements with many props and children.

In the next lesson, we will talk about a little helper method, that eases some of the pain.

Quiz

1. What JavaScript language construct is used to implement virtual DOM elements in React?
2. What field is used in React to set a class for the elements?
3. How are interactions implemented in React?

Lesson 1 - Element Factory

In the previous chapter, we explained how you define React elements with plain JavaScript objects. There isn't much to them, but they are a bit cumbersome to work with, primarily because many of the required keys are often empty or always have the same values.

In this short chapter, we'll learn about a way to get rid of this boilerplate code.

React provides you with a helper function called `React.createElement()`. It adds `$$type` and `ref` attributes to your element definitions every time you call it.

A Simple Element

In the previous lesson, this was how we created an element manually:

react-from-zero/00-object-elements.html

```
var anotherElement = {
  $$typeof: magicValue,
  ref: null,
  type: "p",
  props: {
    children: "A nice text paragraph."
  }
};
```

However, if we used the factory function the code is reduced to this:

react-from-zero/01-element-factory.html

```
var anotherElement = React.createElement(
  "p",
  null,
  "A nice text paragraph."
);
```

This is a more concise (and less error-prone) way to define the same element.

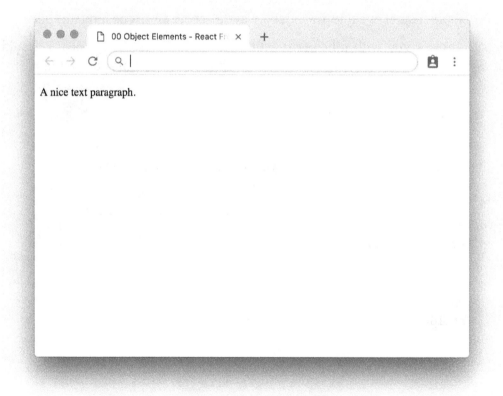

Simple Element

The createElement function takes three arguments.

1. The type of the element we want to create, in this case, a "p".

2. The `props` of the element, things like event handlers or styles. It must be `null` if no `props` are used.
3. The `children` of the element. While children are also `props` React also allows to add them via an extra parameter.

A Complex Element

The more complex example we used in the last chapter would look like this:

react-from-zero/01-element-factory.html

```
var reactElement = React.createElement(
  "h1",
  {
    className: "abc",

    style: {
      textAlign: "center"
    },

    onClick: function () {
      alert("click");
    }
  },
  "Hello, world!"
);
```

Now we use the `props` parameter to define a `style` a `className` an `onClick` event handler.

And if we were to expand the `reactElement` generated by `React.createElement`, the object looks exactly as before:

react-from-zero/00-object-elements.html

```
var reactElement = {
  // This special property will be checked by React to ensure this
  // object
  // is a React element and not just some user data
  // React.createElement() sets it for you
  $$typeof: magicValue,

  // This will also be checked by React. We will be talking about
  // references later, but if you're not using them, this has to be
  // set to null and not undefined
  ref: null,

  // This defines the HTML-tag
  type: "h1",

  // This defines the properties that get passed down to the element
  props: {
    // In this example there is just a single text node as child
    children: "Hello, world!",

    // a CSS class
    className: "abc",

    // styles can be passed as object literals
    // React uses camelCase instead of dashed-case (like CSS/D3 do)
    style: {
      textAlign: "center"
    },

    // event handlers can be added as properties, too
    // React uses synthetic events to try to normalize browser
    // behavior
    onClick: function (notYourRegularEvent) {
      alert("click");
    }
```

```
  }
};
```

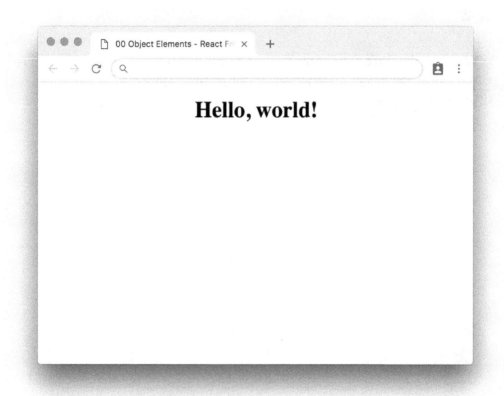

Complex Element

Wrap Up

The factory function `React.createElement()` is a much more concise way to define React element objects. Using `React.createElement` especially shines with simple elements that don't have much configuration (which is the lion's share of most applications).

Some React developers even save `React.createElement()` into a shorter identifier like h, so they can call it directly without much typing and without the need of JSX, which we will talk about in the next chapter.

Quiz

1. What are the three arguments the `React.createElement()` function accepts?
2. What does the `React.createElement()` function return?
3. What does the `React.createElement()` add that we need to do manually when using element objects.

Lesson 2 - JSX

When I hear people complain about React, it's mainly due to **JSX**, the non-standard syntax extension created for writing markup in JavaScript.

If you've used other frameworks like Vue or Ember, you are probably used to template languages like HTMLBars. These are languages with their own semantics and syntax embedded into JavaScript with strings.

The React team went in a different direction: **they tried to use JavaScript directly** to create markup, but also added a JSX as **syntax extension** to the mix. So you can still use your JavaScript know-how, but also use a syntax that more closely resembles HTML.

JSX Compilation

The drawback here is that **it needs an extra compile step** to run in a browser. Which is the second frequent complaint about React: people think they can't use it without an extra build step.

While this is technically true (if you're going to use JSX), there are ways to use JSX compilers like Babel, directly in the browser with a ‹script› tag.

Babel is a **JavaScript compiler**; it is used to compile *new JavaScript features* down to an older version of JavaScript, so that the new features can be used in older browsers that don't implement them natively.

In this case, it **compiles down JSX to regular JavaScript function calls** (using the React.createElement() function we discussed in the last chapter).

Because Babel itself is JavaScript (which runs in the browser) we can include the Babel compiler into our app by adding a ‹script› tag and then instructing Babel to compile our JSX/JavaScript code.

Here we see the Babel stand-alone version, which is created to run in browsers, included via a ‹script› tag from the *Unpkg* content delivery network:

react-from-zero/02-jsx.html

```
<script src="https://unpkg.com/@babel/standalone/babel.min.js">
```

 A content delivery network, short CDN, is a service that provides hosting for content. Unpkg, for example, mirrors the NPM registry and makes the NPM packages available via HTTP, so no extra tooling is required to use them.

If you use the stand-alone version of Babel in the browser, you have to write your JSX and JavaScript inside a ‹script type="text/babel"› tag. By specifying the type of text/babel we're telling the Babel compiler that we want it to compile this code for us (which means we'll gain the benefit of the extra features it supports, i.e. JSX).

A Simple Element

So lets start with our simple element example again:

react-from-zero/02-jsx.html

```
var anotherElement = <p>A nice text paragraph.</p>;
```

This would be compiled down to our simple element example from the factory element lesson.

react-from-zero/02-jsx.html

```
anotherElement = React.createElement(
  "p",
  null,
  "A nice text paragraph."
);
```

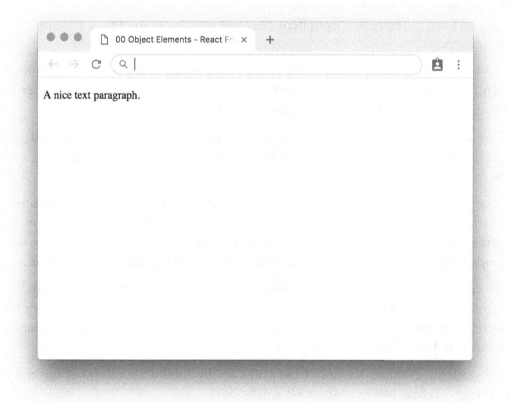

Simple Element

Take a look at the top paragraph code example again - we have ‹p› tags in our JavaScript code! This syntax is supported by the Babel compiler.

The JSX tags will be converted to JavaScript function calls to React.createElement().

The key idea of what's going on here is that **we are simply using the JSX syntax as a shorthand for the JavaScript `React.createElement()` call.**

 Technically, the default configuration of JSX is to call the `React.createElement()` function, however this could also be configured to call a different function if you wanted to.

The *tag name* will become the first, or `type`, parameter of the function, so different tags don't call different functions here, they just supply different `type` parameters to the same function.

One of the powerful features of JSX is that we can compose, not only "primitive" HTML elements, but we can also create our *own* component elements. In order for JSX to support that, there are two cases for the element *tag name*:

If the *tag name* is `lowercase` it will be **passed as a string to the function call**, the function will then try to create a regular VDOM element (as in our example, with the `p` element).

If the *tag name* is `UpperCase` it will be **passed as a *variable* to the function call**, a variable of the same name as the *tag name*. If no such variable exists in the current scope, you get an error. This feature is used to create elements from custom *components*, one major feature about which we will talk about in a later lesson.

The *content* of the element can be another element or, in our case, text. This will be passed into the third, or `children`, a parameter of the function. This allows you to create nested elements like we are used to in HTML. I will tell you about nested elements in the following lesson.

In this simple example, we didn't use `props` so the second parameter of the call to the `React.createElement()` function will be `null`.

A Complex element

The more complex example from the last chapter with many `props`, would look like this in JSX:

react-from-zero/02-jsx.html

```
var reactElement = (
  <h1
    className="abc"
    style={{ textAlign: "center" }}
    onClick={function() {
      alert("click");
    }}
  >
    Hello, world!
  </h1>
);
```

And it would be compiled to this:

react-from-zero/02-jsx.html

```
reactElement = React.createElement(
  "h1",
  {
    className: "abc",
    style: { textAlign: "center" },
    onClick: function() {
      alert("click");
    }
  },
  "Hello, world!"
);
```

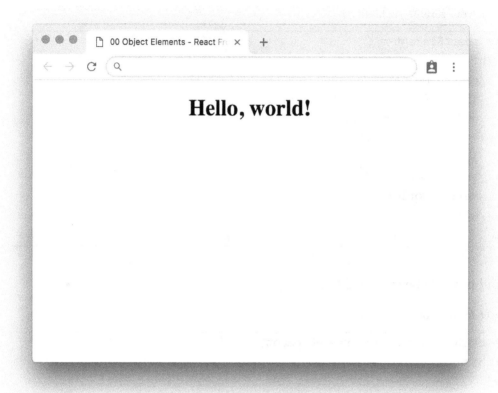

Complex Element

Here you can see that the props were converted to a props object and placed into the second parameter of the React.createElement() function call.

You should also notice **how curly braces are used to embed JavaScript directly into JSX**.

For example, look at the style attribute above:

```
style={{textAlign: "center"}}
```

Notice that we have two curly braces. Why is that?

In this case, we have an inner, plain JavaScript object:

```
{
  textAlign: "center";
}
```

and the syntax in JSX is to use curly braces to define a JavaScript attribute:

```
style={/* javascript here */}
```

We can create a prop with a string value like we do in HTML, by adding `propName="value"`. In this case a string prop is created and added to the object that is passed to the `React.createElement()` function call.

You can also use all other JavaScript values, like objects, numbers, booleans, variables, functions etc. You just have to wrap them in curly braces like this `propName={function() {}}`.

This feature also works with the `content` of your element, or your `children` if you like. For example, if we had a `loggedIn` variable, we could use JavaScript logic to either render a "logged-in" greeting element or a "Please sign in!" element:

<h1>{loggedIn ? ("Hello" + userName + "!") : "Please sign in!"}</h1>

Because JSX tags are just function calls to the `React.createElement()` function, you can store what they return and pass it around like you would with other JavaScript values. **JSX is, after all, just JavaScript**.

Wrap Up

In this lesson we learned about JSX, one of the core technologies that ease markup creation in React code. It makes markup visible in the rest of the code and especially helps when creating small elements.

We learned how to create elements with it and how to embed regular JavaScript into the markup to add custom logic.

We saw that **JSX is nothing more than a different function-call-syntax** and that it can even be used in a browser if you include a stand-alone version of Babel before, so **you don't have to set up a whole build chain** to make your first steps with React and JSX.

In the next lesson we will learn how to **nest elements**, because what is a web application that just can render flat lists of elements?

Quiz

1. Which extra tool is needed to run JSX code?
2. To what JavaScript construct is a JSX element compiled to?
3. How can we execute regular JavaScript inside JSX?

Lesson 3 - Nested Elements

In the last chapter, we learned that JSX **simplifies the creation of markup in JavaScript**.

In this chapter, we will see a powerful feature of JSX: **nesting elements in other elements**.

Nesting with pure JSX

We already learned that the content of an element will be pushed into the `children` argument of a call to the `React.createElement()` function. (To be precise, the content will end up as the third argument to `React.createElement()`.)

The following JSX:

```
<p>text</p>
```

Will be compiled to:

```
React.createElement("p", null, "text");
```

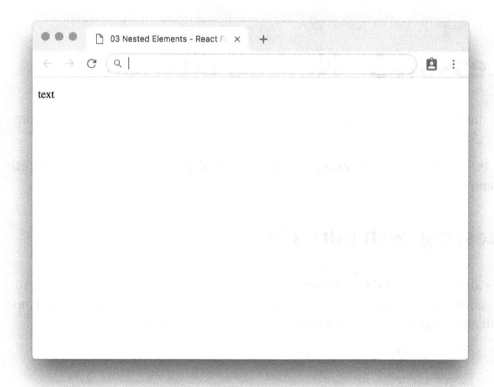

Paragraph Element

Now the interesting part: **this also works if the nested element is another element**:

```
<p>
  <strong>Text</strong>
</p>
```

Will end up as:

```
React.createElement(
  "p",
  null,
  React.createElement("strong", null, "Text")
);
```

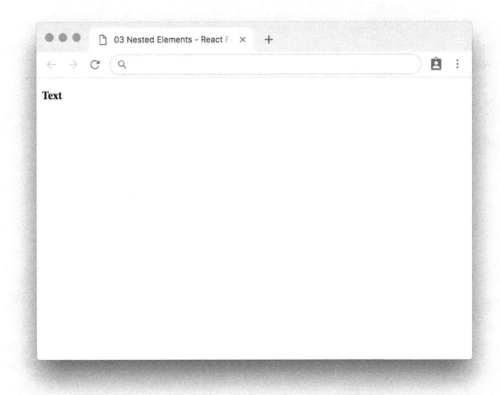

Strong Paragraph Element

You can already see how unwieldy it would be if you built your whole app by calling the element-factory `createElement` directly without using JSX.

It also works for multiple `children` **and** mixed types of `children`:

```
<p>
  Hello, <strong>World</strong>!
</p>
```

Becomes:

```
React.createElement(
  "p",
  null,
  "Hello, ",
  React.createElement("strong", null, "World"),
  "!"
);
```

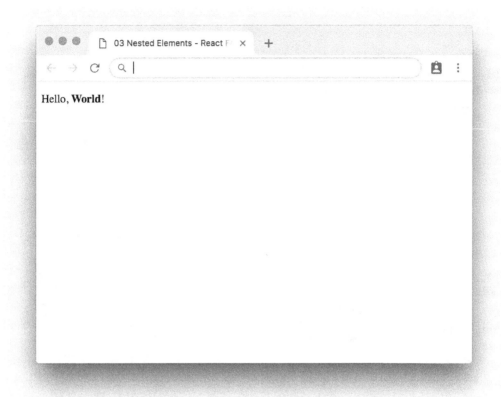

Strong Paragraph Element 2

Here the behavior is a bit different. The child elements didn't end up as an array in the same argument, **they became the subsequent arguments**:

- The string "Hello, " became the third argument
- The <strong> element became the fourth argument
- The string "!" the fifth argument

Nesting with JavaScript

As we learned in the last chapter, you can also **insert your regular JavaScript into JSX** and it will be executed as you would expect.

This feature can be used to call a function or calculate values as nested elements right in JSX.

To do this, we **wrap the JavaScript in curly braces {}**:

react-from-zero/03-nested-elements.html

```
var myClass = "abc";

function myText() {
  return "world";
}

// JavaScript insertion has the same syntax in attributes as in normal
// text or elements
reactElement = (
  <div className={myClass}>
    <h1>Hello {10 * 10}</h1>
    <h2>{myText()}</h2>
  </div>
);
```

The above code will render a DOM that is as if we wrote the HTML:

<div class="abc"> <h1>Hello 20</h1> <h2>world</h2> </div>

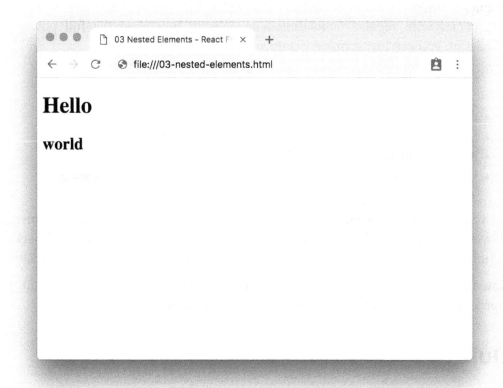

Nested Elements

 The JavaScript in the curly braces {} **must be an** *expression*. This means it needs to evaluate to a *value*.

Statements, like `if`, `switch` or `while`, are not allowed as the first keyword after the opening brace. If you need conditional logic, you *can* use the ternary operator, as in: `{ booleanVal ? "it was true" : "it was false" }`

Wrap Up

This chapter illustrated one of the areas where JSX really shines.

It simplifies the creation of complex element structures without the loss of flexibility that comes with regular templating languages. If you need the full power of JavaScript, you can just sprinkle it onto your JSX.

In the last lessons, we learned:

- the basics of React
- how React elements are plain JavaScript objects at their core
- how they interact with each other and
- how JSX can be used to create DOM structures for React applications.

We've also learned that JSX can be used to simplify the work of creating elements. However, unlike a regular templating language, JSX always allows us to fall-back to full-blown JavaScript whenever we need more complex logic to structure our UIs.

Now that we understand elements we can move to a higher level and talk about the bread and butter of every React application: **Components**

Quiz

1. What do nested JSX elements compile to?

2. Where do multiple nested elements end up in the compiled call to the

`React.createElement()` function?

3. Can JavaScript be used inside JSX' curly braces?

Lesson 4 - Components

Now that we know the ins and outs of *elements*, we can move to **components**, which make up the main selling point of React.

Components allow encapsulating **elements** and **behavior** for *reuse* in our application.

Functional Components

The most basic version is a **functional component**. They are simply a function with `UpperCase` name.

 Functional components are sometimes also called **stateless components** because they can't have their own state.

Let us take a simple example with some `data` and nested elements:

react-from-zero/04-components.html

```
var data = "world";
var reactElement = (
  <div>
    <h1>Hello</h1>
    <h2>{data}</h2>
  </div>
);
```

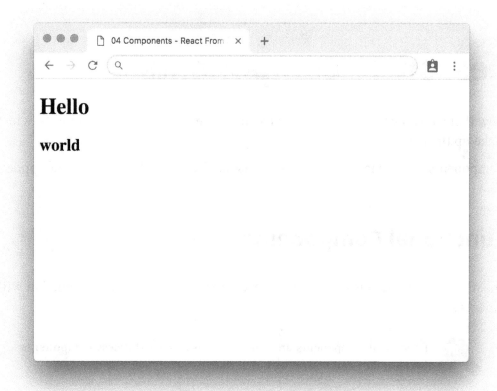

Nested Elements

We could now use reactElement somewhere to render the example, but the data it uses isn't encapsulated **and** if we wanted to use reactElement within the JSX of another element, we would have to wrap the variable reactElement in curly braces (we'll remove this restriction below).

One improvement we could make would be to rewrite the example with a simple function:

```
function myElement() {
  var data = "world";
  return (
    <div>
      <h1>Hello</h1>
      <h2>{data}</h2>
    </div>
  );
}
```

This does solve the problem of encapsulating data and sometimes for simple elements you might see React developers write an element this way.

But this still doesn't allow us to use the component inside JSX without JavaScript interpolation (that is, using myElement in JSX, as defined above, would require the syntax of: { myElement() } instead of being able to use a "custom tag").

If we write it like this, with an UpperCase function name, we can use this function name **as a new JSX tag**.

react-from-zero/04-components.html

```
function MyComponent() {
  var data = "world";
  return (
    <div>
      <h1>Hello</h1>
      <h2>{data}</h2>
    </div>
  );
}
```

If we use an UpperCase first letter, JSX won't pass a string as the first/type argument to the React.createElement() function but **a reference**. This is great news because it lets us *compose* components. To illustrate, when using the lowercase tag <text>:

<text>X</text> becomes React.createElement("text", null, "X")

but when using the uppercase tag <Text>:

`<Text>X</Text>` becomes `React.createElement(Text, null, "X")`

Notice the missing `""`. Instead of a string, a variable named `Text` is used as the first argument. Why does this help us? Because `Text` can be a component (or function) that wraps complex behavior.

In the case of `MyComponent`, we can now **use it as a tag in our JSX**. For example, if we had the code:

```
<div className="greeting">
  <div>Here is a greeting:</div>
  <MyComponent/>
</div>
```

It would render into a DOM that looks like:

```
<div class="greeting">
  <div>Here is a greeting:</div>
  <div>
    <h1>Hello</h1>
    <h2>world</h2>
  </div>
</div>
```

The benefit here is enormous: we can craft progressively more sophisticated pages while encapsulating complexity within component trees.

In React, as a loose rule-of-thumb we'll keep each component in it's own file. Then, when we need to use the component we'll `import` it.

Typically we'd use a variable with the same name as the component. However, in the case of conflicts we can rename the variable when we `import`. Them, we can use this new variable name in JSX. Just keep in mind that the new name also has to start with an `UpperCase` letter!

Requirements for The Component Variable

As we just learned, an `UpperCase` tag like `<Text>...</Text>` is passed as a variable name into the `React.createElement()` function, there are two requirements this first/type argument (`Text`, in this case) must satisfy:

1. There must be a variable in scope with that exact name
2. The variable must be a function that returns an element, an array of elements or `null`

Returning a List of Elements

If our component returns more than one element (and we don't want to wrap it into an extra `<div>` element), we can return the elements in an array or in a `<React.Fragment>` (discussed below).

react-from-zero/04-components.html

```
function MyComponent() {
  var data = "world";
  return [<h1 key="hello">Hello</h1>, <h2 key="data">{data}</h2>];
}
```

The array version requires us to use a `key` prop for every element.

 The `key` prop is used by React to **determine the position of multiple elements in one array**. If we update one of these elements and keep the key the same, React doesn't need to replace every element from the array in the virtual DOM when it checks for changes.

Notice that another downside of returning an array is that **we have to keep track of commas**.

If we use `<React.Fragment>` instead of an array, we don't have to keep track of `key` props *or* use commas, it **works as a regular element without rendering any extra DOM elements** to our page that would bloat our markup.

react-from-zero/04-components.html

```
function MyComponent() {
  var data = "world";
  return (
    <React.Fragment>
      <h1>Hello</h1>
      <h2>{data}</h2>
    </React.Fragment>
  );
}
```

Wrap Up

Functional components provide an easy way to create custom elements that integrate nicely with JSX. They allow for encapsulation of component-specific data or elements and for reuse of these in multiple places of one or even multiple applications.

Functional components are the simplest type of components. They don't hold their own state and are completely controlled via the props they get from their parent elements. To make them more usable for us, we will talk about props in the next lesson.

 How do you like *React from Zero* so far?

Would you take a minute and let us know what you like about the book and what you think could be better? We'd love to hear from you.

Click here[3]

Quiz

1. What improvement do *functional components* bring over regular functions that return elements?

---

[3]https://www.fullstackreact.com/r/react-from-zero-satisfaction/

2. What's the major constraint of a component name?
3. What do arrays of element need to be updated efficiently by React?

Lesson 5 - Props

In the last lesson, we learned how to create simple component that encapsulated elements and data. In this lesson, we will find out **how to pass data from the outside into a component.**

Call-Site Props

We've already used props when we worked with elements in the earlier chapters. For example, when we set `className` or `style` we're using props.

```
<p className="black-text" style={{ fontSize: 42 }}>
  Text
</p>
```

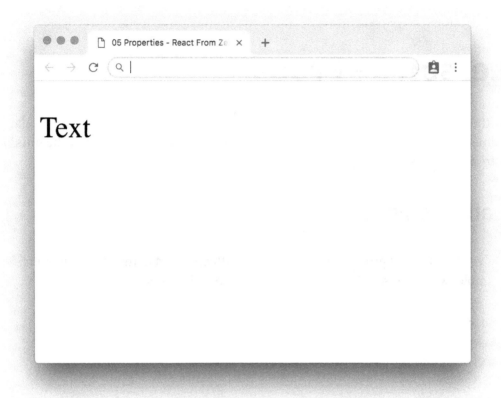

Text Element

The props of this example get compiled to a props-object, which will look like this:

```
{
  className: "black-text",
  style: {
    fontSize: 42
  }
}
```

This object is passed into the `React.createElement()` function as the second/props argument (or `null` when no props are used).

Now, what happens if we pass props to a custom component, one that we've created?

Here is some JSX where the custom component MyComponent is used and it receives two props: className and customData, which both have a string value:

react-from-zero/05-properties.html

```
var reactElement = <MyComponent className="abc" customData="world" />;
```

 Remember, we can pass much more than strings to props. We could also pass functions, numbers, objects or other types into the props – as long as we use curly braces

You probably notice that these props in JSX look a lot like attributes in HTML. We call these key/value pairs: *call-site props* (e.g. customData="world" above). That is these are the props at the site that calls our component in the JSX.

Definition-site Props

But the next question is: **how can we use props inside our components?** It looks like this:

react-from-zero/05-properties.html

```
function MyComponent(props) {
  return (
    <div className={props.className}>
      <h1>Hello</h1>
      <h2>{props.customData}</h2>
    </div>
  );
}
```

Every **functional component** receives the props object as first argument. It's the same props object that is passed to the React.createElement() function as second argument.

So, for example, using the "call-site props" above, MyComponent would render the equivalent of:

```
<div class="red-text">
  <h1>Hello</h1>
  <h2>world</h2>
</div>
```

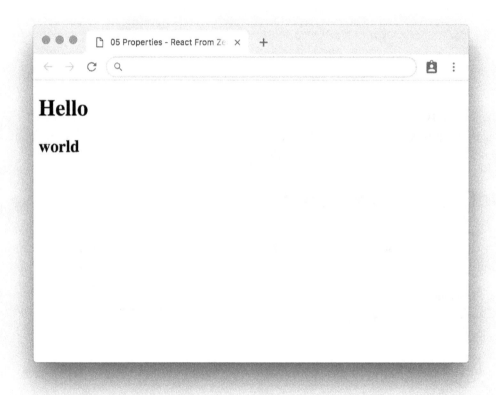

Props in Component

Default Props

It is also possible to define default props by setting the defaultProps attribute of the component to an object. Its keys are the name of the props we want defaults for and its values are, well, the actual values.

react-from-zero/05-properties.html

```
MyComponent.defaultProps = {
  customData: "default-data",
  className: "default-class"
};
```

Customizing Components with Props

Using props allows us to re-use components and pass configuration options. By passing function props, we can even trigger special behavior.

Consider this example where we create a custom styled Button component with a size prop.

```
// Definition
function Button(props) {
  var style = {
    color: "white",
    backgroundColor: "red"
  };

  switch (props.size) {
    case "s":
      style.height = 30;
      style.width = 50;
      break;
    case "l":
      style.height = 50;
      style.width = 100;
      break;
    default:
      style.height = 40;
      style.width = 75;
  }
```

```
  return (
    <button style={style} onClick={props.onClick}>
      Click Me!
    </button>
  );
}

// Usage
<Button
  size="s"
  onClick={function() {
    alert("!!!");
  }}
/>
<Button
  onClick={function() {
    alert("!!!");
  }}
/>
<Button
  size="l"
  onClick={function() {
    alert("!!!");
  }}
/>
```

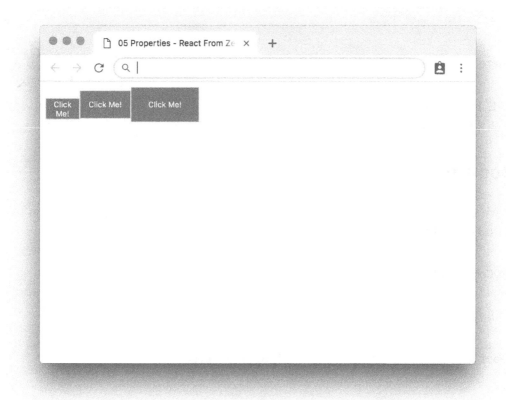

Props in Component

In this examples we pass two props:

- `size` and
- `onClick`

The `size` prop is used in the `switch` above. Depending on the value of `props.size` we will set a different `height` and `width` on the `style` object. Since the `switch` has a `default` branch, the `size` prop isn't even required to use the component.

The `onClick` prop is a **function** and can do whatever we want (!). In this case we're going to `alert("!!!")`, but this pattern of passing a function to a prop is very powerful and will be used a lot in React apps.

Special Cases

There are two special cases for `props` usage:

1. Boolean props
2. Props spreading

Boolean Props

If we don't define a value for a prop, it will get the value `true`. This is to be in line with HTML behavior and allows for terser syntax in component design.

```
<MyComponent active />
```

Will become:

```
React.createElement(MyComponent, { active: true });
```

Props Spreading

It is also possible to **spread** an object onto an element. This allows for a dynamic amount of `props` passed to an element right in JSX without the need to fall back to JavaScript syntax.

react-from-zero/05-properties.html

```
var props = {
  className: "abc",
  customData: "world"
};


reactElement = <MyComponent {...props} />;
```

This translates to:

```
React.createElement(MyComponent, {
  className: "abc",
  customData: "world"
});
```

Often, when creating a custom component, we don't want to pass all props down to the children. For this, we have to add some logic to decide what to pass dynamically. With **props spreading** this can be achieved in an elegant way.

 There are reserved names for props: key and ref. They have special meaning for React and won't be accessible inside of a component later. key is used when rendering an array, to tell React which child is which and ref is used as a non-global alternative to the id prop we know from HTML, but we'll talk about this in another chapter.

Wrap Up

In this chapter, we learned how to use props on elements and inside of our custom components. Now we can create components that can be controlled from the outside.

Besides state, which we will learn later, props are one of the most fundamental concepts in React.

props with non-function values are used **to pass state from parents to children** and function props, triggered via props like onClick, are used **to pass state up to the parent again**.

There is no such thing as two-way-binding in React, we have to manually **pass down** our data via props and **pass up** new data via function calls.

In the next chapter, we will learn about prop-types, a way to check if the values we passed into our props have the correct type.

Quiz

1. What are props used for in React?
2. Does React use **two-way-binding**?
3. What do function props accomplish in React?

Lesson 6 - Prop Types

Now that we know how to use props in our custom components, it would be nice to prevent users of these components from using invalid values. That is, a certain prop may only work properly if it is passed a `String` or a `Component`.

There exist multiple solutions for this problem, like static typing[4] with Flow[5] or TypeScript[6], but those solutions involve essentially using another programming language which requires a compile-to-Javascript step, which is something we'd like to avoid.

Instead of checking the types of the props at compile time, we can implement a solution in JavaScript by checking at *runtime*. React has a library for type checking at run time called **prop types**.

In this book, we will talk about the prop-types solution, because it works without adding new syntax to the language.

Prop-types are an **optional** part of React and come in their own NPM package (since version 16).

We can include them with a `<script>` tag from the Unpkg CDN like this:

react-from-zero/06-property-types.html

```
<script src="https://unpkg.com/prop-types@15.6.1/prop-types.js">
```

Runtime Type Checking

The main idea of prop-types is that **we add a `propTypes` attribute to our component function**. Then, React will use these `propTypes` to validate the `props` passed in to this component.

---

[4]https://stackoverflow.com/questions/1517582/what-is-the-difference-between-statically-typed-and-dynamically-typed-languages

[5]https://flow.org/

[6]https://www.typescriptlang.org/

This validation will happen when the code that passes the props is executed, hence **runtime type checking. We have to run the code** in some fashion that triggers the type check to see if everything is correct.

Prop-Types for Functional Components

Lets look at a simple example of a **functional component** function:

react-from-zero/06-property-types.html

```
function MyComponent(props) {
  return (
    <div className={props.className}>
      <h1>Hello</h1>
      <h2>{props.customData}</h2>
    </div>
  );
}
```

The component passes its customData prop down to the <h2> elements children prop. We know this expects a value of type string, so we add a prop-type for this prop to the component.

react-from-zero/06-property-types.html

```
MyComponent.propTypes = {
  // React supplies us with a bunch of types, like string
  customData: PropTypes.string
};
```

We set the attribute propTypes to an object that contains our validators.

- Keys of the propTypes object are the names of the prop we want to check
- Values are the actual *validators*. These come from the prop-types package

The prop-types packages comes with many validators for basic types, like `string`, `number`, `bool`, `func`, `array` etc. It also has React specific types like `node` or `element` and allows for the check of custom object types and much more. You can find the list of validators in the documentation[7]

In this case we simply check if the `customData` prop is of type `string`, if we would pass a `number` into it we would get the following warning at runtime:

Warning: Failed prop type: Invalid prop `customData` of type `number` supplied to `MyComponent`, expected `string`.

Complex Example

Lets look at a more practical example of how **prop-types** could be used in an actual component.

react-from-zero/07-property-example.html

```
function DateSpan(props) {
var date = props.date,
  day = date.getDate(),
  month = date.getMonth() + 1,
  year = date.getFullYear();

  return (
    <span>
      {day}.{month}.{year}
    </span>
  );
}
```

react-from-zero/07-property-example.html

```
DateSpan.propTypes = {
  date: PropTypes.instanceOf(Date).isRequired
};
```

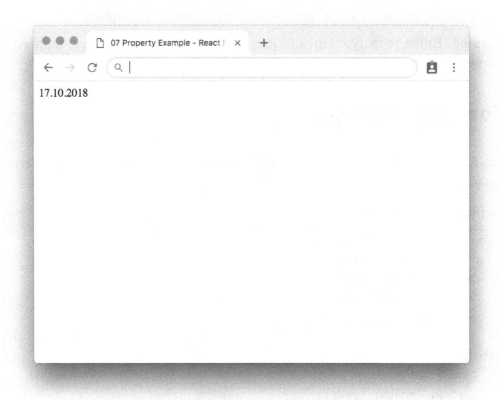

DateSpan Component

- DateSpan component takes a date object
- date prop isRequired
- date prop **has to** be an instance of the built-in JavaScript Date class

The component takes day, month and year out of the date prop and creates a text representation of it that can be rendered into the DOM.

Wrap Up

Now we know how to create our own custom components and also how to validate the props passed into them with the help of **prop-types**.

In the next lesson we talk about how components can be *nested*.

Quiz

1. At what time are prop-types checked?
2. Are prop-types part of React?
3. Do prop-types check or alarm you of code that isn't reached?

Lesson 7 - Nested Components

In the last few chapters, we learned the basics of `props`, which allows us to pass values from parent components down into child components.

But one thing is missing: we haven't talked about *how* to nest components into each other.

Call-Site Nesting

Let's go back to using `React.createElement` for a minute (the "call-site") and explore how nesting works here (then we'll move back to JSX).

To refresh, let's create a `<p>` element with an `<em>` element and a text element as children.

```
<p>
  <em>Hello</em>, world!
</p>
```

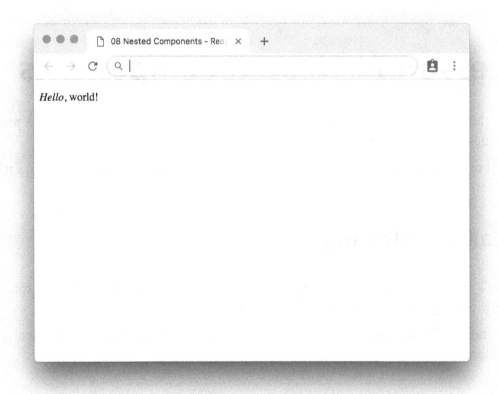

Hello, World!

This would translate to the plain JavaScript version:

```
React.createElement(
  "p", // first
  null, // second
  React.createElement("em", null, "Hello"), // third
  ", world!" // fourth
);
```

Here, we add a *child* element as content to another (*parent*) element and the *parent* element will render it as a child *node* into the *virtual* DOM tree.

The two elements in the content of the <p> element end up in the **third** and **fourth** argument of the `React.createElement()` function. That's all we need to do to nest elements.

Definition-Site Nesting

The question is now, how do we nest something inside a custom component we've created?

For this, we need the `children` prop. It is basically a reference to the "content" of our component.

In the example above we used a `<p>` element and added two elements to its content, let's do this with a custom component called `<RedText>`:

```
<RedText>Hello, world!</RedText>
```

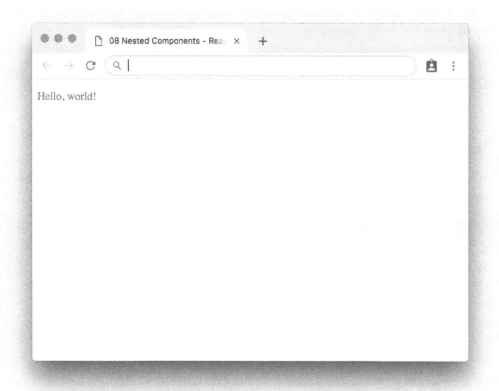

Hello, World!

The implementation of this component could be as follows:

```
function RedText(props) {
  return <p style={{ color: "red" }}>{props.children}</p>;
}
```

So what is happening here?

RedText...

- uses a `<p>` its base element
- styles it with an in-line style
- passes the `children` prop into the `<p>` elements content

The last point is the crucial part; it passes `children` on to another element **without looking at it**. `children` will have a reference to the `"Hello, world!"` string from above, but we could pass anything here (including another component), `RedText` will only care about how it implements its behavior and leave everything else to the element it passes its `children` to.

Nesting Components into Components

As you can imagine, this doesn't only work with elements. We can **pass components into components** too.

Take the following example:

react-from-zero/08-nested-components.html

```
  function Item(props) {
  return <li>{props.children}</li>;
}

// This component wraps its children into an <ul> element
function List(props) {
  return <ul>{props.children}</ul>;
}

// If the <List> is created without children it gets a default child
List.defaultProps = {
  children: <Item>Empty</Item>
};

// now we render two <List>s, without and with Items
var reactElement = (
  <div>
    <List />
    <List>
      <Item>First</Item>
      <Item>Second</Item>
      <Item>Third</Item>
```

```
    </List>
  </div>
);
```

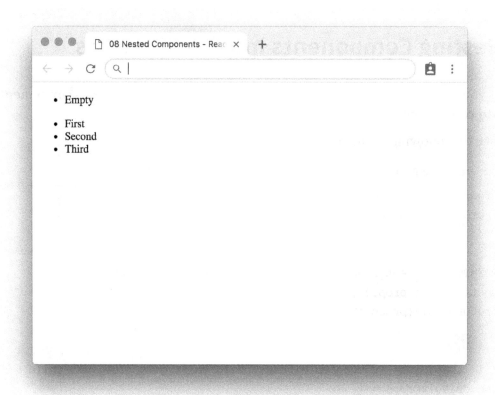

Hello, World!

The Item component wraps a `<li>` element and the List component wraps an `<ul>` element. They both pass their children to these elements.

The List component even defines `defaultProps` for its `children`. This is possible because the `children` prop is a prop like every other.

We could now refactor the List or Item component to have different styles, and the rest of the application wouldn't need to be changed because everything is encapsulated.

The children prop is a bit special because **it can have different types**. If a component gets passed only **one** child its children prop will hold a reference to **this one** child, but if a component gets passed multiple children, the children prop will hold a reference to an opaque data-structure that holds all the child elements, a child collection. Also, the children prop can be undefined if nothing has been passed to the component.

For this problem React offers the React.Children object, which comes with a few handy utility methods like .map(), .count() or .toArray(). They allow working with the contents of the children prop without worrying about its actual content.

Wrap Up

In this chapter we learned about another feature of React: **nesting components**. Now we can not only create a whole UI with elements but also modularize parts of it (for re-use and encapsulation) into components that can work with other components via the children prop.

The fact that props are one of the most important parts of React still holds true, because children also are just props passed down from parent elements.

Since we now know how to build up whole UIs and pass data around via props, in the next lesson, we will learn about another component type: the **class component**.

Quiz

1. How are nested elements accessed inside a component?
2. How are children different from props?
3. Can children have different types?

Lesson 8 - Class Components

Now that we've learned what we can do with **functional components**, it is time to add *state*!

Functional components are fine for a large part of our application, but somewhere we have to store state.

Remember, functional components only have their props to control their behavior and these props have to come from the parent. If we think this chain of props passed down to the end, we notice that there has to be a place where the first props are created somehow.

Class Components

To create a stateful component, we have to create a **class** instead of a simple **function**.

 Class Components are also called **stateful components**, because they can have their own state, but not all class components have state, so this name is missleading.

For example, say we wanted to create a component which keeps track of a counter and we click on a button to increment that counter. Look at this component:

```
function Counter(props) {
  return (
    <div>
      <span>{props.count}</span>
      <button onClick={props.onClick}>+ 1</button>
    </div>
  );
}
```

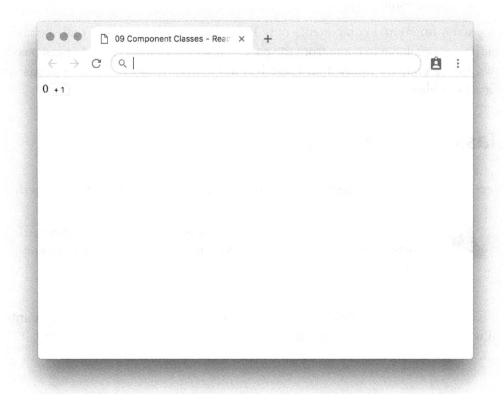

Counter Component

Above, we display the count prop and use the onClick prop to pass data up. But parent has to handle the click **and** pass a updated count down to the Counter. There is no way to store the value of the counter (the *state*) in this component.

If we define Parent as functional component, we can create the count variable and the onClick handler that increments this variable; and then pass them into the props of our Counter component, but we would have no way to tell React that we need to re-render these two components.

```
function Parent(props) {
  var count = 0;

  function handleClick() {
    count++;
    // ...?
  }

  return <Counter count={count} onClick={handleClick}/>
}
```

To fix this, a class component is the way to go here, because **it can store its state without the need of a parent**:

```
var Counter = createReactClass({
  getInitialState: function() {
    return { count: 0 };
  },

  handleClick: function(event) {
    this.setState(function(prevState) {
      return { count: prevState.count + 1 };
    });
  },

  render: function() {
    return (
      <div>
        <span>{this.state.count}</span>
        <button onClick={this.handleClick}>+ 1</button>
      </div>
```

```
    );
  }
});
```

That exploded into quite a lot of code, so let's start from the beginning.

The createReactClass() Function

First, we use the createReactClass() function, this is the ES5 way of creating class components with React. In version 16 of React it was moved to its own package, but it can be included with a simple <script> tag like this:

react-from-zero/09-component-classes.html

```
<script src="https://unpkg.com/create-react-class@15.6.3/create-react-c\
lass.js">
```

This function returns a new component class. Classes in JavaScript are also functions, so **we can change functional components to class components transparently.** Simply set an UpperCase variable name for it an use it as a JSX element.

The render() Method

The createReactClass() function takes a config object that needs to define some functions. The most important one being the render() method. As you might have noticed, this function looks suspiciously like our functional component function from above and you're right with that!

When using class-based components the render() method doesn't receive props via argument, but instead we need to use this.props to access the props (however, this isn't shown in this current code example). The same idea goes for state - it won't be passed down via argument, but needs to be accessed via this.state:

```
// ...
render: function() {
  return (
    <div>
      <span>{this.state.count}</span>
      <button onClick={this.handleClick}>+ 1</button>
    </div>
  );
}
// ...
```

`this` will be **the current instance of the component**, when inside the `render()` method, so we can also access all the other things we passed to the `createReactClass()` function in the config object, like the custom method `handleClick`. This method is neither a prop nor part of the state, so we can access it with `this.handleClick`.

The getInitialState() Method

The next interesting part is the `getInitialState()` method. It will be called when the an instance of the the component is created, right before the first call to the `render()` method.

```
// ...
getInitialState: function() {
  return { count: 0 };
},
// ...
```

It needs to `return` a value that defines the state of our component. In this example we use an object with a `count` attribute. This value is then available in the `render()` method via `this.state.count`.

When you're getting started with React, the convention is that state is typically an object, as it is here.

An object is convenient because you can store several key-value pairs. However, state can be anything you'd like: a number, a string, or a more sophisticated object.

As you can see, the return value of the `getInitialState()` method becomes `this.state`.

Interaction

We want interaction in our counter, so we've created a `<button>` and added our custom `handleClick` method as an `onClick` handler.

```
// ...
handleClick: function(event) {
  this.setState(function(prevState) {
    return { count: prevState.count + 1 };
  });
},
// ...
```

The `handleClick` method is now where the **update** happens. It receives an `event`, which we don't care about in this example.

Next, it calls to a `setState()` method - we didn't define this method, but React provides it for us!

The setState() Method

The `setState()` method is the center of state management in React. Every time you call it, your `render()` method is called with an updated `this.state`.

The setState() method can be called with an object or with a callback function, like we did in the example.

If we call it with an object, this object gets (shallow[8]) merged with the current object inside this.state.

This is useful when we don't depend on the previous state. For example, when we sent a request to a server a received an error. We don't need to check the previous state, we know the request isn't pending anymore and we got an error message we can display, all independent from what happened before.

```
this.setState({loading: false, error: "404 - File not found."});
```

If we call it with a callback function, the callback receives the previous state as an argument and needs to return the new value that is merged with this.state, just like getInitialState() did.

 Only call the setState() method with an object if the new state doesn't depend on the previous state.

If you find yourself writing things like {count: this.state.count + 1} you need to switch to the callback version and use the first/prevState callback argument instead of this.state for your calculations!

In our example, we use the callback version, because we increment the counter based on the previous state. This version is asynchronous, it tells React that we want to update state and give it a callback to do so. React will execute this callback function some time in the future.

When the callback has been executed, our render() method will be called again, in this method this.state will have the values we updated in the callback.

---

[8]https://reactjs.org/docs/state-and-lifecycle.html#state-updates-are-merged

This model of interactions is called unidirectional dataflow and is a core concept of React. It stands in contrast to the two-way-binding known from other frameworks.

It is probably the most foreign concept in React and puts off newcomers quite a bit. That said, it's more explicit and makes it easier to reason about data-flow in complex applications, because the "framework magic" is reduced to a minimum.

Example With Extras

Here another example with more things we know from functional components:

react-from-zero/09-component-classes.html

```
var MyComponent = createReactClass({
  // used for type-checking of the properties
  // same as with the component function
  propTypes: {
    color: PropTypes.string
  },

  // this method sets default values for missing properties
  // it will be called by React
  // before the components gets mounted into the DOM
  getDefaultProps: function() {
    return { color: "green" };
  },

  // this method sets the initial state for the component
  // it will be called by React
  // before the components gets mounted into the DOM
  // if this method is missing, this.state will be undefined
  getInitialState: function() {
    // The state can be any JavaScript value, often it is an object
    return { times: 0 };
```

```
},

// this method handles all the clicks on the <span> element
handleClick: function() {
  // setState() can be called with an object that contains the new
  // state. Normally this triggers a call of render(), but React can
  // batch multiple calls and defer the render() call (make the call
  // asynchronous). To prevent this, setState can take a callback
  // instead.

  // This can lead to unexpected behavior, if we rely on this.state
  // or this.props for our calculations
  // this.setState({times: this.state.times + 1})

  // The callback version doesn't have this problem, it gets the
  // right state and props at time of the update
  this.setState(function(prevState, props) {
    return { times: prevState.times + 1 };
  });
},

// this method will be called by React
// after the component got mounted into the DOM
// also every time this.setState() was called
// it's like the component function from before
// but without a props argument
render: function() {
  // using the prop given by the creator of this component
  // properties are now in this.props instead of the props argument
  var style = { color: this.props.color };

  // returning an element with a click-handler and the props and
  // state values. state is stored in this.state
  return (
    <span onClick={this.handleClick} style={style}>
      Clicked {this.state.times} times
```

```
    </span>
  );
 }
});
```

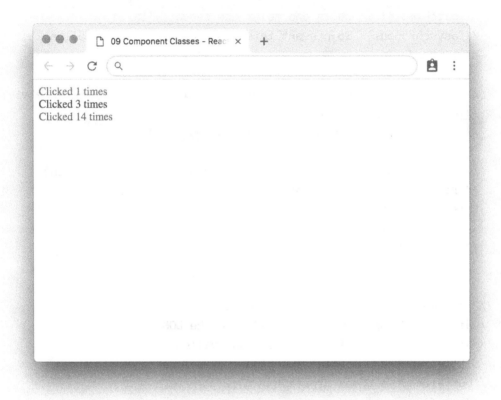

Counter Component with Extras

- The propTypes can simply be defined as attribute of the config object passed to createReactClass
- The defaultProps need to be defined as getDefaultProps() method.

Wrap Up

In this chapter we learned another essential: **class components**

Every React application with interaction needs to hold state somewhere. Often class components don't render elements directly, but

- use functional components for display purposes and
- pass down the state that needs to be displayed via `props`.

In the next chapter we will learn about some useful methods we can add to our component classes to handle React specific events: **lifecycle methods**

Quiz

1. How is the library called that allows to use classes without ES2015?
2. What is the main addition of **class components** over **functional components**?
3. What are the two versions of the `setState()` method?

Lesson 9 - Lifecycle Methods

The **class components** we learned about in the last chapter, allow us to use another feature of React: **lifecycle methods**

These are methods of a component class with special names that are called on specific events. We can think of them as event handlers.

In this lesson we will learn about the two most important lifecycle methods:

- `componentDidMount()` and
- `componentWillUnmount()`

.

The `componentDidMount()` Method

The first method that is used very often in React apps is `componentDidMount()`. If we define it in our component class, React will call it right after the first time our `render()` method was called. The name means that the component was mounted into the DOM.

The most important use-cases for this method are:

- fetching asynchronous data
- setting up event listeners

Here's an example:

```
var AsyncHelloWorld = createReactClass({
  getInitialState: function() {
    return { data: null };
  },

  componentDidMount: function() {
    var self = this;
    setTimeout(function() {
      self.setState({ data: "Hello, world!" });
    }, 2000);
  },

  render: function() {
    var data = this.state.data;
    if (!data) return <p>Loading...</p>;
    return <p>{data}</p>;
  }
});
```

Before the timeout triggers:

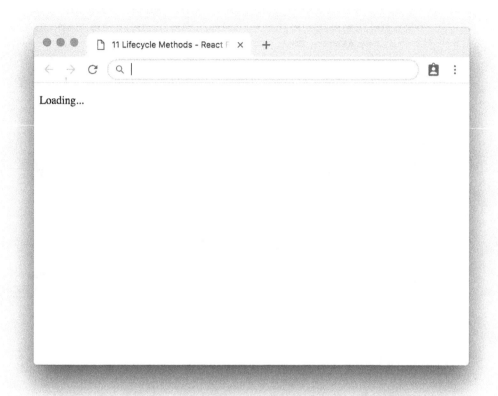

AsyncHelloWorld Component Loading

After the `timeout` triggers:

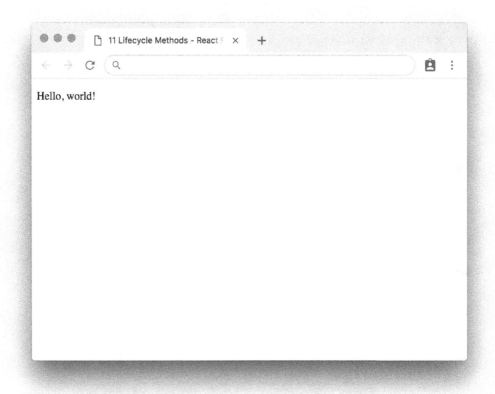

AsyncHelloWorld Component

1. The initial `state` is {`data: null`}
2. The `render()` method checks the state and `returns` a Loading indicator
3. React calls the `componentDidMount()` method, which simulates asynchronous data retrieval with a timeout
4. The `setState()` method is called after 2000 milliseconds to update the `state` with the *received* data
5. The `render()` method is called again, this time with the new `state`, so no loading indicator is shown

You might notice in componentDidMount that we have the line var self = this; – what's going on there?

Well, if you recall, this in JavaScript refers to the enclosing function. This means that if we were to call this.setState within the setTimeout callback function, setState would be undefined (because this is the setTimeout function, **not** our component instance AsyncHelloWorld).

So we define a local variable self, which allows us to refer to the component instance within the callback.

If you're using ES6, there is a language feature called the "fat arrow"[9] which helps us avoid this extra self variable.

This is the most basic way that componentDidMount() is used. Other ways could include some setup that needs to take place before the component is usable, like connecting to WebSockets, etc.

The componentWillUnmount() Method

This will be the last method of our component class that will be called by React right before our component gets removed from the DOM.

Its main use-case is **cleanup**. You can think of it as a destructor from OOP.

Here an example that shows how the:

- componentDidMount() method and the
- componentWillUnmount() method play together.

---

[9]https://developer.mozilla.org/en-US/docs/Web/JavaScript/Reference/Functions/Arrow_functions

```
var AsyncCounter = createReactClass({
  getInitialState: function() {
    return { count: 0 };
  },

  incrementCounter: function() {
    this.setState(function(prevState) {
      return { count: prevState.count + 1 };
    });
  },

  interval: null,
  componentDidMount: function() {
    this.interval = setInterval(this.incrementCounter, 100);
  },

  componentWillUnmount: function() {
    clearInterval(this.interval);
  },

  render: function() {
    return <p>Count: {this.state.count}</p>;
  }
});
```

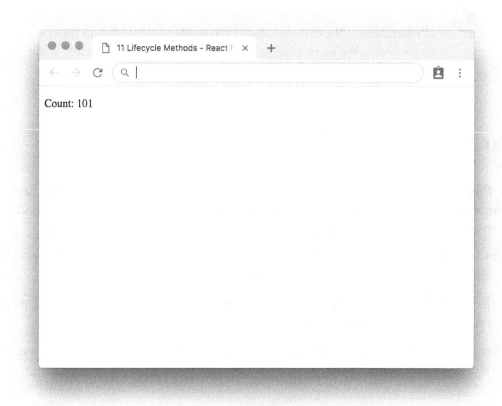

AsyncCounter Component

1. The component gets mounted to the DOM and renders a `<p>Count: 0</p>`, because the initial `state` is {`count: 0`}.

2. React calls the `componentDidMount()` method, which sets an interval that increments `state.counter` every 100 milliseconds and stores a handle to it inside a class attribute for later use.

3. Every time the interval executes, the `setState()` method is called, which will lead to a `render()` method call after the state was changed.

4. Before the component gets removed from the DOM, React calls:

- the `componentWillUnmount()` method, which in turn will call
- the `clearInterval()` function on the handle we stored.

This example also shows, that data can simply be stored into class attributes of components (like `this.interval`) and doesn't have to live in the `state` or the `props`. We do this for data that doesn't affect the rendering of the component.

Wrap Up

In this chapter we learned the two most important lifecycle methods of React, `componentDidMount()` and `componentWillUnmount()`, and how they can be used to react to events that React itself generates when dealing with our components.

They can be used to retrieve data from asynchronous data-sources or to setup event-handlers for events that aren't React element or component related.

In the next lesson, we will wrap up **Part I** of this book with an example application that uses all of the features we learned.

After that, we should be able to do about 80% of the day-to-day tasks that arise when developing a React application.

Quiz

1. When is the `componentDidMount()` lifecycle method called?
2. When is the `componentWillUnmount()` lifecycle method called?
3. What are use-cases for the `componentDidMount()` method?

Part II

In the second part of this book we will talk about additional topics. Things that may only be of interest in 20% of the time.

Most of the work with React is building simple components and nest them together, but once in a while you need to restructure your code, improve quality or use some advaced techniques to solve a particulare problem. This is where **Part II** comes into play.

In this part you will learn:

- What other lifecycle methods exist and when to use them
- How to refactor element and component structures
- How to integrate third party libraries
- How to write automated tests

Lesson 10 - Example App

Now that we know how **class components** work, we can finally write our first app.

Our first app is a *Pomodoro timer*. It has interactions, asynchronous events and works with the dependencies we already know.

Pomodoro Timer

A Pomodoro timer[10] helps divide time into chunks.

There are two types of time-chunks:

1. Work time, which has a duration of 25 minutes
2. Pause time, which has a duration of 5 minutes

The use-case is as follows:

- The user starts the timer; then they work for 25 minutes
- The timer switches automatically to pause and the user has to pause for 5 minutes
- The timer switches back to work and the whole cycle restarts
- The user can stop the timer at any time

Here's what our app will like in the end:

---

[10]https://en.wikipedia.org/wiki/Pomodoro_Technique

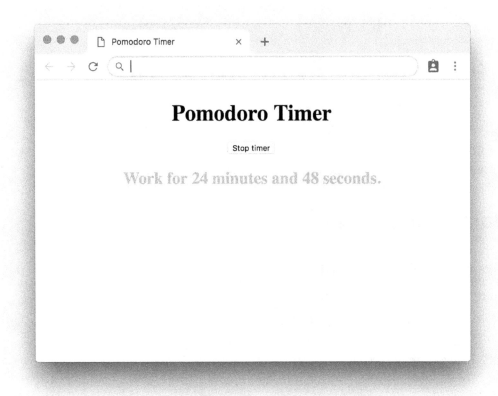

The Pomodoro App

Implementation

We need to create three components for this app.

- PomodoroApp - The root component of our app
- Timer - The component that counts down for a specific duration
- Idle - The component that is displayed when the timer isn't running

The HTML structure of our app looks like this:

```
<div
  style="display: flex; flex-direction: column; align-items: center;">
  <h1>Pomodoro Timer</h1>
  <button>Start timer</button>
  <h2>No Timer Running.</h2>
</div>
```

In the different states of our app, only the styles and text of the elements will change. Let's go through the components "bottom-up".

First, the Idle component, because it's the simplest of all. Next, the Timer component, because it's more complex than the Idle component and needed by the last one we'll implement: the PomodoroApp component.

The Idle Component

The Idle component is the simplest component in this app: it displays text and a button. It doesn't even have to handle the button click event itself so it can be a **functional component**.

example-app/idle-component.html

```
var Idle = function(props) {
  return (
    <React.Fragment>
      <button onClick={props.onStart}>Start timer</button>
      <h2>No Timer Running.</h2>
    </React.Fragment>
  );
};
```

We pass the onClick event to the onStart prop and wrap the two elements into a React.Fragment component, so they are rendered without any wrapping element into the DOM later.

The <Idle> component looks like this:

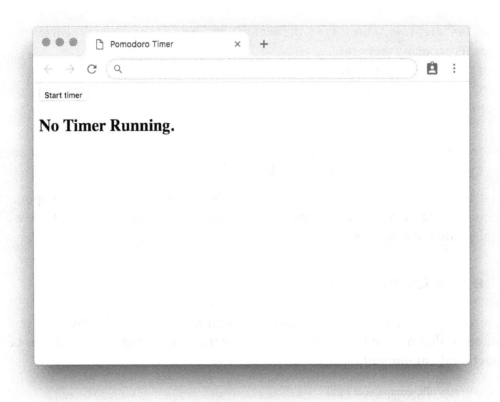

The Idle Component

The `Timer` Component

The most interesting component. It handles the actual timer count-down, so it has to be a **class component**.

Let's build it up method by method. We'll start by creating the `Timer` component with just a `render()` method.

```
var Timer = createReactClass({
  render: function() {
    return <span>Timer</span>;
  }
});
```

This component needs to display a count-down, so let's add a method that does this:

```
var Timer = createReactClass({
  countDown: function() {
    var onFinish = this.props.onFinish;
    this.setState(function(prevState) {
      var secondsLeft = prevState.seconds - 1;

      if (secondsLeft < 1) return onFinish();

      return { seconds: secondsLeft };
    });
  },

  render: function() {
    return <span>Timer</span>;
  }
});
```

The `countDown()` method tries to decrement `state.seconds` every time it's called, and if the value is below 1, it calls the `props.onFinish()` callback.

We haven't set an initial `state` yet. Without this, no `state.seconds` would be available. So let's add our initial state:

```
var Timer = createReactClass({
  getInitialState: function() {
    return { seconds: this.props.minutes * 60 };
  },

  countDown: function() {
    var onFinish = this.props.onFinish;
    this.setState(function(prevState) {
      var secondsLeft = prevState.seconds - 1;

      if (secondsLeft < 1) return onFinish();

      return { seconds: secondsLeft };
    });
  },

  render: function() {
    return <span>Timer</span>;
  }
});
```

The getInitialState() method is called by React **before rendering the first time**. We use the minutes props to calculate the seconds we need.

Our timers run in multiples of one minute, so using minutes as a unit in the props makes it easier to configure our component.

However, because we will count-*down* per second, then we want to store seconds in the state (vs. minutes).

The next step is to wire up the countDown() method.

```
var Timer = createReactClass({
  getInitialState: function() {
    return { seconds: this.props.minutes * 60 };
  },

  interval: null,
  componentDidMount: function() {
    this.interval = setInterval(this.countDown, 1000);
  },
  componentWillUnmount: function() {
    clearInterval(this.interval);
  },

  countDown: function() {
    var onFinish = this.props.onFinish;
    this.setState(function(prevState) {
      var secondsLeft = prevState.seconds - 1;

      if (secondsLeft < 1) return onFinish();

      return { seconds: secondsLeft };
    });
  },

  render: function() {
    return <span>Timer</span>;
  }
});
```

To call the `countDown()` method we use an *interval* that calls the method every second, or 1000 milliseconds. We also need to start this interval somewhere. To do this, Reacts lifecycle-methods are perfect.

The `componentDidMount()` method is called right after the first render so we can use it to call the `setInterval()` function, which starts our interval. We also need to store a *handle* (a reference) to the interval in a place that can be read later so we can stop the timer. We store this handle in `this.interval`.

React calls the componentWillUnmount() method before the component gets removed from the DOM, so here we can use the clearInterval() function to **stop** our interval. If we didn't call clearInterval(), the countDown() method would continue call the setState() method – even after the instance of the component has already been destroyed.

Now our Timer component is configurable via props and counts down its timer every second until it is removed from the DOM. When the timer gets below 1 second, it executes the onFinish() callback (which we haven't described yet).

The only thing left now is to **display our time**. Just rendering a <span> that doesn't update won't help. So in the render() function, let's add some markup filled with state to finish up our component.

example-app/timer-component.html

```
var Timer = createReactClass({
  getInitialState: function() {
    return { seconds: this.props.minutes * 60 };
  },

  interval: null,
  componentDidMount: function() {
    this.interval = setInterval(this.countDown, 1000);
  },
  componentWillUnmount: function() {
    clearInterval(this.interval);
  },

  countDown: function() {
    var onFinish = this.props.onFinish;
    this.setState(function(prevState) {
      var secondsLeft = prevState.seconds - 1;

      if (secondsLeft < 1) return onFinish();

      return { seconds: secondsLeft };
    });
```

```
    },

    render: function() {
      var seconds = this.state.seconds;
      var minutes = Math.floor(seconds / 60);
      seconds = seconds % 60;

      return (
        <React.Fragment>
          <button onClick={this.props.onStop}>Stop timer</button>
          <h2 style={{ color: this.props.color }}>
            {this.props.title} for {minutes} minutes and {seconds} second\
s.
          </h2>
        </React.Fragment>
      );
    }
});
```

This example shows the complete `Timer` component. It calculates `minutes` and `seconds` from the `state.seconds` to display them in a user-friendly way. Since we used `setState()` to update the `seconds` the `render()` method is called every time the `countDown()` method was called.

We use a `title` and `color` prop to make the display more flexible because we want to use this component two times:

1. As a Work-Timer
2. As a Pause-Timer

We also add a `<button>` that executes the `onStop` callback, when clicked. This callback allows us to tell the parent that we want to stop the timer before it reached its end.

The two versions of the `<Timer>` component we use look like this:

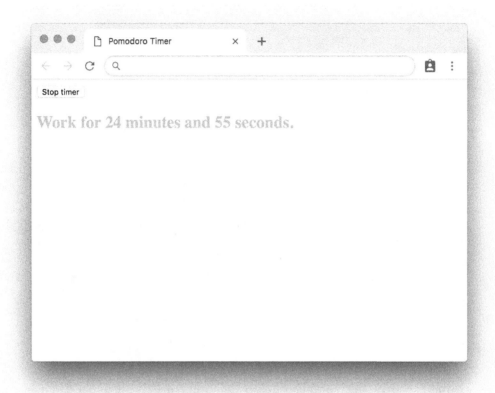

Work Timer Component

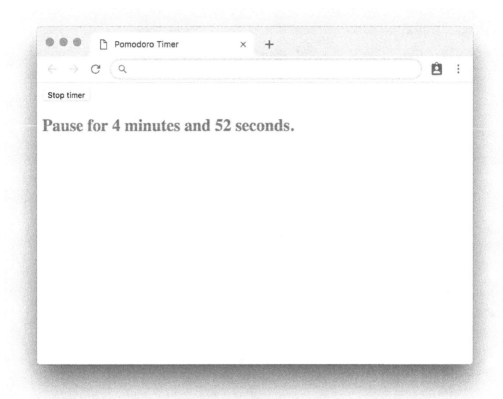

Pause Timer Component

The PomodoroApp **Component**

The PomodoroApp component handles the transition between the states of the timer, so it needs to be a **class component**.

We start with an empty component again.

```
var PomodoroApp = createReactClass({
  render: function() {
    return <span>Pomodoro Timer</span>;
  }
});
```

The PomodoroApp component keeps track of two different types of state.

- The current state of the timer.
- The count of work timers that finished.

Let's add them to our empty component:

```
var PomodoroApp = createReactClass({
  IDLE: 0,
  WORK: 1,
  PAUSE: 2,

  getInitialState: function() {
    return {
      count: 0,
      timerState: this.IDLE
    };
  },

  render: function() {
    return <span>Pomodoro Timer</span>;
  }
});
```

The current state of the timer can be one of three states, IDLE, WORK and PAUSE. So we define them as fields in our class, the UPPER_CASE writing implies they are constants. The count of work timers that finished merely is a number.

Then we have to set the initial state in the getInitialState() method. The app starts in an idle state without any timer running, so we use this.IDLE.

Because no work timers have finished yet, we can also use 0 as the starting count.

Next, we need to integrate our `<Idle>` and `<Timer>` components, because they handle all the interaction.

```
var PomodoroApp = createReactClass({
  IDLE: 0,
  WORK: 1,
  PAUSE: 2,

  getInitialState: function() {
    return {
      count: 0,
      timerState: this.IDLE
    };
  },

  render: function() {
    var count = this.state.count;
    var timerState = this.state.timerState;

    var timerElement = <Idle onStart={this.handleWork} />;

    if (timerState == this.WORK)
      timerElement = (
        <Timer
          key="work"
          title="Work"
          color="orange"
          minutes={25}
          onFinish={this.handlePause}
          onStop={this.handleIdle}
        />
      );

    if (timerState == this.PAUSE)
      timerElement = (
```

```
        <Timer
          key="pause"
          title="Pause"
          color="green"
          minutes={5}
          onFinish={this.handleWork}
          onStop={this.handleIdle}
        />
      );

    return (
      <div
        style={{
          display: "flex",
          flexDirection: "column",
          alignItems: "center"
        }}
      >
        <h1>Pomodoro Timer</h1>
        {timerElement}
        {!!count && <h2>You worked {count * 25} minutes today!</h2>}
      </div>
    );
  }
});
```

Now our updated render() method uses our other two components.

If the timerState is this.IDLE, we use the <Idle> component and hook its onStart prop up to an event handler that handles the start of a work-timer.

If the timerState is this.WORK, we use the <Timer> component and configure it via props to behave like a work-timer. We also hook-up event handlers for onFinish and onStop events of the <Timer> component, so we can switch to other timerStates when needed.

If the timerState is this.PAUSE, we also use the <Timer> component, but this time configured differently to resemble a pause-timer, we also add the event handlers to switch `timerStates`.

 We use two instances of the `<Timer>` component in the same place.

In one state we configure it as work-timer in another state we configure it as pause-timer. This tells React that we want to reuse the component, but only change the config. We need to supply different `key` props to tell React these are different components that just happen to be in the same place at different times, otherwise React wouldn't reset the `<Timer>` components state when `timerState` changed.

The `<PomodoroApp>` component also has some markup on its own to show a title and use `state.count` to display minutes the user already worked.

We know a Pomodoro working timer always takes 25 minutes, so we can multiply the count by 25 to get the right amount of minutes. The `!!count &&` prevents the `<h2>` from being rendered when `count` is 0.

We can also refactor the component a bit:

```
var PomodoroApp = createReactClass({
  IDLE: 0,
  WORK: 1,
  PAUSE: 2,

  getInitialState: function() {
    return {
      count: 0,
      timerState: this.IDLE
    };
  },

  getTimerElement: function() {
    var timerState = this.state.timerState;

    if (timerState == this.PAUSE)
      return (
        <Timer
```

```
        key="pause"
        title="Pause"
        color="green"
        minutes={5}
        onFinish={this.handleWork}
        onStop={this.handleIdle}
      />
    );

  if (timerState == this.WORK)
    return (
      <Timer
        key="work"
        title="Work"
        color="orange"
        minutes={25}
        onFinish={this.handlePause}
        onStop={this.handleIdle}
      />
    );

  return <Idle onStart={this.handleWork} />;
},

style: {
  display: "flex",
  flexDirection: "column",
  alignItems: "center"
},

render: function() {
  var count = this.state.count;

  return (
    <div style={this.style}>
      <h1>Pomodoro Timer</h1>
```

```
      {this.getTimerElement()}
      {!!count && <h2>You worked {count * 25} minutes today!</h2>}
    </div>
  );
  }
});
```

Now the `getTimerElement()` method handles all our interaction with the two other components. The `render()` method doesn't even know about the `timerState` anymore.

Since we only have a bit of in-line styling on one element here, we can add it as a class field and reference it in the `render()` method via `this.style`, this indirection makes that method a bit more readable.

The only missing parts are the event handlers that get called by the `<Idle>` and `<Timer>` components.

example-app/index.html

```
var PomodoroApp = createReactClass({
  IDLE: 0,
  WORK: 1,
  PAUSE: 2,

  getInitialState: function() {
    return {
      count: 0,
      timerState: this.IDLE
    };
  },

  handleWork: function() {
    this.setState({ timerState: this.WORK });
  },

  handlePause: function() {
    this.setState(function(prevState) {
```

```
      return {
        count: prevState.count + 1,
        timerState: this.PAUSE
      };
    });
  },

  handleIdle: function() {
    this.setState({ timerState: this.IDLE });
  },

  getTimerElement: function() {
    var timerState = this.state.timerState;

    if (timerState == this.PAUSE)
      return (
        <Timer
          key="pause"
          title="Pause"
          color="green"
          minutes={5}
          onFinish={this.handleWork}
          onStop={this.handleIdle}
        />
      );

    if (timerState == this.WORK)
      return (
        <Timer
          key="work"
          title="Work"
          color="orange"
          minutes={25}
          onFinish={this.handlePause}
          onStop={this.handleIdle}
        />
```

```
    );

    return <Idle onStart={this.handleWork} />;
  },

  style: {
    display: "flex",
    flexDirection: "column",
    alignItems: "center"
  },

  render: function() {
    var count = this.state.count;

    return (
      <div style={this.style}>
        <h1>Pomodoro Timer</h1>
        {this.getTimerElement()}
        {!!count && <h2>You worked {count * 25} minutes today!</h2>}
      </div>
    );
  }
});
```

The handleWork() method sets the timerState to this.WORK and is called via the onStart prop of the <Idle> component and the onFinish prop of the <Timer> component, but only when we configure the <Timer> component as pause-timer.

The onStart prop gets called by a press on the start button of the <Idle> component. We execute the onFinish callback if the interval in the <Timer> component goes under 1.

The handlePause() method sets the timerState to this.PAUSE and increments the count, so we can display how many work-timers have finished successfully. We only call it via the onFinish prop of the <Timer> component, if we configured the <Timer> component as a work timer.

We call the onFinish callback if the interval in the <Timer> component goes under 1.

We call the handleIdle() method via the onStop callback of the <Timer> component, which in turn uses its stop button's onClick event. This execution is indifferent to the timer being a work-timer or pause-timer.

Unidirectional Data Flow

The <Timer> component also shows how unidirectional data flow gives you more control about events.

To display the right minutes and seconds in the text **we explicitly set the state** in the countDown() method and then use it in the render() method. **There is no two-way-binding** involved.

This approach allows us to see the whole journey our value takes, and we can apply checks or modify it at any position. For example, we check if the updated value is smaller than 1 and we calculate minutes and seconds from the value before rendering it.

Let's look at a diagram that illustrates this better:

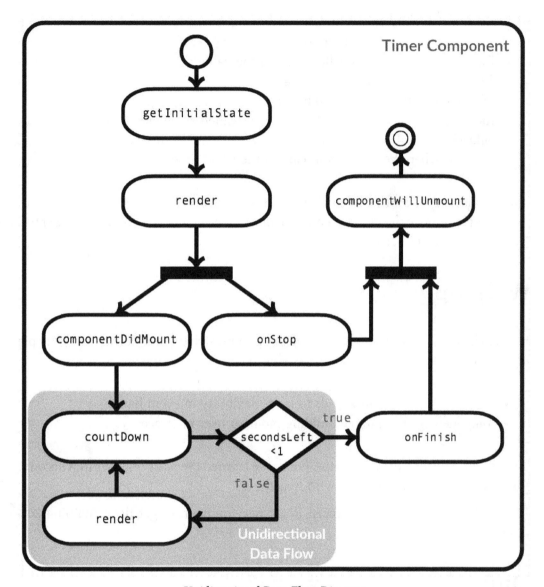

Unidirectional Data Flow Diagram

1. The getInitialState() method is called by React.
2. React renders the component into the DOM for the first time.
3. The componentDidMount() method is called by React; it sets up an interval of 1000 milliseconds.

4. The interval calls the countDown() method; it tries to update the state, if the new value is too low it executes the onFinish() callback.
5. The render() method is called again if the value was bigger than 1. It renders the component with the new state.
6. After 1000 milliseconds we go to 4. again.
7. The componentWillUnmount() method is called by React if the onFinish() callback was called at 4, this allows us to clear the interval so it won't get executed when the component isn't in the DOM anymore.

There is also an onStop() callback we call if the <button> is clicked. This call causes the parent to remove the <Timer> component from the DOM, so our componentWillUnmount() is called by React either way.

Wrap Up

In this chapter, we used knowledge of the previous chapters to create an example application. It illustrated how:

- unidirectional data-flow leads to more flexibility in event handling
- component systems allow building modular user interfaces

This lesson is the end of *Part I* of this book. We learned the basic features that account for 80% of the day-to-day work with React.

In *Part II* we learn about advanced React development, to get the remaining 20% done.

Quiz

1. How is data passed down to children in React?
2. How is data passed up to parents in React?
3. How do we replace two instances of the same component in the same place?

Lesson 11 - More Lifecycle Methods

We already talked about and used the two most essential lifecycle methods in the previous chapters `componentDidMount()` and `componentWillUnmount()`.

The idea with `componentDidMount()` and `componentWillUnmount()` is that we have some code "hooks" which can run at certain points in our component's life. There are a few other *lifecycle methods* and in this chapter, we learn about the rest of them.

While you won't use all of these lifecycle methods in every component, when you need it, you'll be glad they exist.

Here are the four other lifecycle methods:

- `componentDidUpdate()`
- `shouldComponentUpdate()`
- `getDerivedStateFromProps()`
- `getSnapshotBeforeUpdate()`

React calls each of them at a specific time in a components lifecycle, hence the name. Some can even be called multiple times.

The following diagram illustrates when React calls each method:

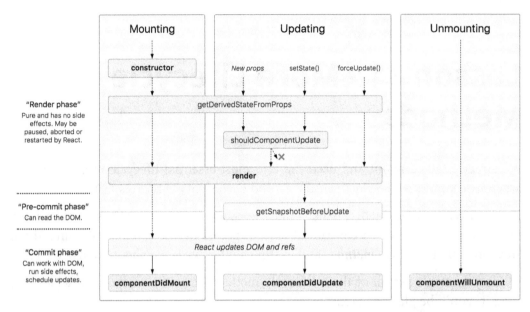

Lifecycle Diagram

Source github.com/wojtekmaj/react-lifecycle-methods-diagram[11].

In the diagram above, each column represents a "render-cycle".

- The *Mounting* cycle runs once on an instance creation of each component.
- The *New Props* cycle runs every time the parent component updates the props.
- The *setState* cycle runs when the setState() method of the component is executed.
- The *forceUpdate* cycle runs when the forceUpdate() method is called.
- The *Unmounting* cycle runs once before React removes the component from the DOM.

The componentDidUpdate() Method

This method lets us add logic after every update to the DOM. We can, for example, check if state or props have changed and issue asynchronous calls to fetch new data from the server.

---

[11]https://github.com/wojtekmaj/react-lifecycle-methods-diagram

React calls this method in the *New Props, setState* and *forceUpdate* cycle.

Here's an example:

```
var Profile = createReactClass({
  getInitialState: function() {
    return { userName: "..." };
  },

  componentDidMount: function() {
    this.fetchUser(this.props.userId);
  },

  componentDidUpdate: function(prevProps, prevState, snapshot) {
    if (this.props.userId !== prevProps.userId) {
      this.fetchUser(this.props.userId);
    }
  },

  fetchUser: function(userId) {
    fetch("/users/" + userId).then(function(user) {
      this.setState({ userName: user.name });
    });
  },

  render: function() {
    return <h2>{this.state.userName}</h2>;
  }
});
```

In this example, we render a `<h2>` element with a `userName`. It's initialized with `"..."` and will be updated after the first mount into the DOM **and** after every update to the `userId` prop with a value fetched from the back-end.

 To prevent infinite-loops, we have to set a *condition* by which `setState()` calls are issued.

The `shouldComponentUpdate()` Method

This method allows us to tell React when the component should update.

- If we `return false` from this method, React won't bother to update the DOM
- If we `return true` React updates the DOM

React calls the method in the *New Props* and *setState* cycle, so it can only stop these two cycles. **It can't stop the first render or the unmounting/removal** of a component.

The primary use-case for this is third-party libraries that render into the DOM directly. We pass props or state to the library, but we don't want React to re-render the target DOM element the library uses to render its elements.

Let's look at this example:

```
var Graph = createReactClass({
  componentDidMount: function() {
    this.renderGraph(this.props.graphData);
  },

  shouldComponentUpdate: function(nextProps, nextState) {
    this.renderGraph(nextProps.graphData);
    return false;
  },

  renderGraph: function(data) {
    var domTarget = document.getElementById(this.props.id);
    // graphLibrary is an imaginary non-React 3rd-party library
    graphLibrary.render(domTarget, data);
  },

  render: function() {
    return <div id={this.props.id} />;
  }
});
```

In this example, we render an empty `<div>` element with an ID. We then use the ID in the `renderGraph()` method to let a third party library render to the `<div>` element.

The `renderGraph()` method gets called by the `componentDidMount()` method, which gets called when the `<div>` element with the ID is in the DOM. It gets also called by the `shouldComponentUpdate()` method, every time the `<Graph>` component gets new props.

Our `shouldComponentUpdate()` method always returns `false`, so the `<div>` element with the new content rendered by the third party library doesn't get overridden by a new empty `<div>` element, but since we call the `renderGraph()` method before that, the third party library can update independently from React.

The `getDerivedStateFromProps()` Method

This method can be used to update a components `state` when new `props` are received. **It has to be a static method**, which means `this` is not available here.

React calls this method in the *Mounting*, the *New Props*, the *setState* and the *forceUpdate* cycle.

The `return` value of this method gets merged with the current `state` of the component.

Let's look at this simple example to illustrate:

```
var Timer = createReactClass({
  getInitialState: function() {
    return { seconds: 0 };
  },
  render: function() {
    return <span>Seconds: {this.state.seconds}</span>;
  }
});

Timer.getDerivedStateFromProps = function(nextProps, prevState) {
  var nextState = {
    seconds: nextProps.minutes * 60
```

```
  };
  return nextState;
};
```

In this example, we use the `minutes` prop to calculate our internal `seconds` state.

The `getDerivedStateFromProps()` method has to be added to the `Timer` class we created, this makes it a static method. In contrast `getInitialState()` and `render()` are regular instance methods that can access `this`.

The `getSnapshotBeforeUpdate()` Method

This method is called right before React updates the DOM with new `state` and `props`, so we can get any UI state, like scroll position, to scroll the component if some dimensions or some elements have changed.

The `return` value will be passed as third argument to the `componentDidUpdate()` lifecycle method.

React calls this method in the *New Props*, *setState* and *forceUpdate* cycle.

In this example, we check if a new item was added to the list right before the render of the component. If it is the case we `return` a value for the scroll position of the list:

```
var ScrollList = createReactClass({
  getSnapshotBeforeUpdate: function(prevProps, prevState) {
    if (this.props.listItems.length > prevProps.listItems.length) {
      var list = document.getElementById(this.props.id);
      return list.scrollHeight - list.scrollTop;
    }

    return null;
  },

  componentDidUpdate: function(prevProps, prevState, snapshot) {
    if (snapshot !== null) {
      var list = document.getElementById(this.props.id);
```

```
      list.scrollTop = list.scrollHeight - snapshot;
    }
  },

  render: function() {
    return <div id={this.props.id}>{/* listItems */}</div>;
  }
});
```

Here, the `snapshot` value is passed to the `componentDidUpdate()` method as the third argument and can be used to manipulate the DOM directly after React rendered the component.

In this case, we update the scroll-position of the `<div>` element our component rendered.

The `forceUpdate()` Method

This method isn't a lifecycle method, but we can used it inside event-handlers or lifecycle methods. It's pre-defined on a class component object and can be used like the `setState()` method, but without any arguments.

We can use the `forceUpdate()` method if we need to re-render based on events of a third party library. Normally we store the data needed for rendering inside `this.state`, but sometimes we don't want to maintain multiple versions of the data. This requires us to tell React when we need a new render.

Here'a simple example of the `forceUpdate()` method:

```
var Example = createReactClass({
  componentDidMount: function() {
    var self = this;
    library.onNewData(function() {
      self.forceUpdate();
    });
  },
  render: function() {
    var dataList = library.getDataList();

    return (
      <ul>
        {dataList.map(item => <li>{item.title}</li>)}
      </ul>
    );
  }
});
```

Wrap Up

In this chapter, we learned about the remaining lifecycle methods and how they allow us to hook into React's render pipeline and how they give us more flexibility in the implementation of our components.

Quiz

1. Will a call to the forceUpdate() method trigger the shouldComponentUpdate() lifecycle method?
2. What is a use-case for the getSnapshotBeforeUpdate() lifecycle method?
3. In which lifecycle methods can we do asynchronous calls to fetch data?

Lesson 12 - Refactoring Components

Refactoring is a big part of the software development process, and **React's component system helps us with this task.**

Most of the time, **one component maps to one file**, and we can change their implementation as we wish (as long as we don't change the props interface).

Changing Implementations

Take this example which renders a table that shows a list of people in rooms:

react-from-zero/12-component-refactor.html

```
function ViewBefore(props) {
  return (
    <table>
      <thead>
        <tr>
          <th>Room</th>
          <th>People</th>
        </tr>
      </thead>
      <tbody>
        {props.rooms.map(function(room, k) {
          return (
            <tr key={k}>
              <td>{room.name}</td>
              <td>{room.people}</td>
            </tr>
          );
```

```
      })}
    </tbody>
  </table>
 );
}


// The component has a simple props-interface
ViewBefore.propTypes = {
  rooms: PropTypes.arrayOf(PropTypes.shape({
    name: PropTypes.string.isRequired,
    people: PropTypes.number.isRequired
  })).isRequired
}
```

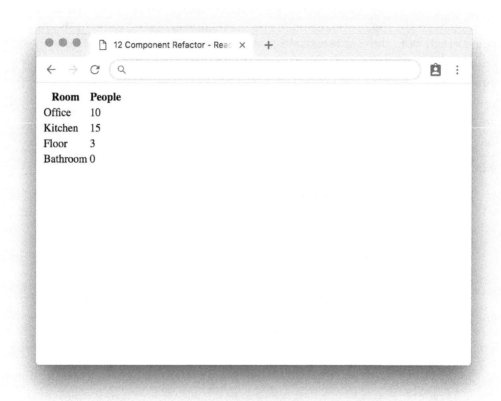

Before Refactor

This component expects an array of room-objects as defined in its propTypes. It renders this array with the help of a ‹table› element and its corresponding child-elements.

Because this component has defined its propTypes we can change its implementation without any changes to the call site of the component.

This means that we can use any component with the same propTypes in its place.

For example this one:

react-from-zero/12-component-refactor.html

```
// We switch out the implementation with something more complex
function ViewAfter(props) {
  return (
    <div>
      {props.rooms.map(function(room, k) {
        var barStyle = {
          display: "inline-block",
          background: "lightgrey",
          width: room.people * 25
        };
        return (
          <div key={k}>
            {room.people > 0 ? (
              <span style={barStyle}>{room.people} People</span>
            ) : (
              <span>0 People</span>
            )}
            <span> in {room.name}</span>
          </div>
        );
      })}
    </div>
  );
}
// We keep the props-interface the same
ViewAfter.propTypes = {
  rooms: PropTypes.arrayOf(PropTypes.shape({
    name: PropTypes.string.isRequired,
    people: PropTypes.number.isRequired
  })).isRequired
}
```

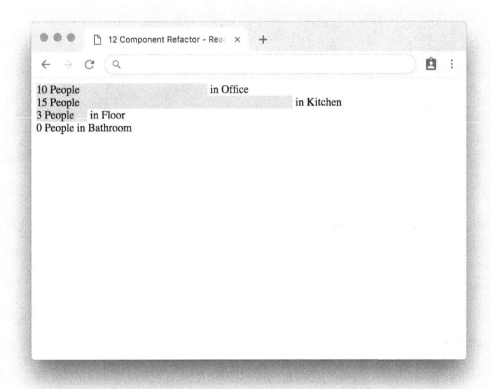

After Refactor

This component uses the same props as the first version but renders them as a simple bar chart.

This also works with dynamic examples:

react-from-zero/12-component-refactor.html

```
// We could also switch it with something more dynamic
var ViewDynamic = createReactClass({
  // We still keep the props-interface the same
  propTypes: {
    rooms: PropTypes.arrayOf(PropTypes.shape({
      name: PropTypes.string.isRequired,
      people: PropTypes.number.isRequired
    })).isRequired
  },

  getInitialState: function() {
    return { currentRoom: 0 };
  },

  componentDidMount() {
    var component = this;
    var props = this.props;

    this.interval = setInterval(function() {
      var currentRoom =
        component.state.currentRoom < props.rooms.length - 1
          ? component.state.currentRoom + 1
          : 0;
      component.setState({ currentRoom: currentRoom });
    }, 1000);
  },

  componentWillUnmount() {
    clearInterval(this.interval);
  },

  render: function() {
    var room = this.props.rooms[this.state.currentRoom];

    return (
```

```
        <span style={{ color: this.state.color }}>
          Room <b>{room.name}</b> has <b>{room.people}</b> People.
        </span>
      );
    }
  });
```

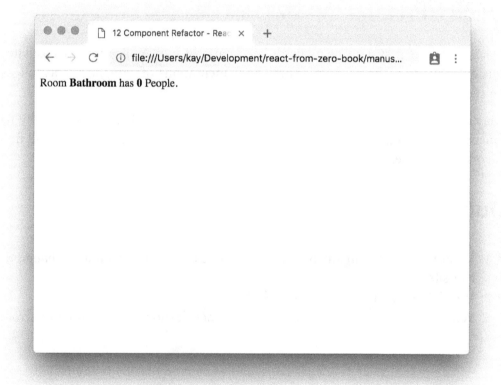

Dynamic Refactor

This component also has the same props interface defined in its propTypes, but it only renders a text description for one room at a time and switches to another room every second with an interval.

These components all require the same props, but they have different sizes in the UI.

We won't get any warnings or exceptions, but we can end up with UI glitches if the dimensions are too different, so it's always important to check if the refactored component fits in its place.

Wrap Up

Reacts component system helps us to keep parts of our application encapsulated. This encapsulation allows us to change implementations of components as long as we keep the props interface the same.

It is not a silver bullet though. UIs aren't just defined by their data, but also by the concrete representation of it, so we need to check if the refactored versions still fit in the overall scheme.

Quiz

1. What parts of a component can't be changed if we don't want to change the call-site?
2. Which library can help us with refactoring?
3. What problems can arise, even if our code doesn't show any warnings or errors?

Lesson 14 - Refs

This chapter is about a React feature that allows us to interact with the DOM directly: **refs**.

 refs are a specific React feature and not an abbreviation for **references**. When we write about the React feature, we'll use the abbreviation **ref**. When we write about **references**, we're talking about using variables to aliasing objects.

Most of the time we model our interactions with the **unidirectional data-flow** pattern provided by React via props and state, but sometimes we need direct access to the DOM elements, for example when we want to **change focus in forms** or **integrate with third party libraries** that don't know about React.

A **ref** is a reference to a DOM element we can store in a variable for later use.

 Using refs is not **not** the typical architecture for the bulk of our React app. Refs are considered a "last resort" when we must directly manipulate the DOM.

Creating Refs

To create a **ref** we have to supply a ref prop to the element we want to reference later. The value of this prop can be:

- A callback, that gets the DOM elements reference as the first argument
- A ref object, created via the React.createRef() method

Callback Refs

Let's look at an example with a *callback*:

```
var App = createReactClass({
  button: null,
  handleRef: function(button) {
    this.button = button;
  },

  handleClick: function() {
    console.log(this.button);
  },

  render: function() {
    return <button ref={this.handleRef} onClick={this.handleClick} />;
  }
});
```

When the <App> component is mounted in the DOM, React calls the render() method.

When we render the <button>, React calls the handleRef() method, that we supplied to the ref prop of the <button>.

In the handleRef() method **we store the reference** (which React passes to our method as the first argument).

React will call this method every time a new rendering of the <App> component replaces our <button> element in the DOM.

In handleClick, when we click the button, we log the current element stored in this.button.

If we hover with the cursor over the logged element in the console, we see that it is the <button> we clicked, as seen in this screenshot:

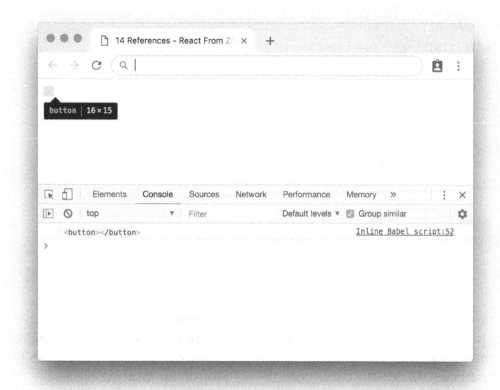

Button Element

The callback version is good if we need to do some extra work with our reference when it changes, but most of the time we want to store the reference and update it when it changes and nothing else.

Ref Objects

For this React supplies us with a extra method `React.createRef()`, so let's look at an example of it:

```
var App = createReactClass({
  button: null,
  getInitialState: function() {
    this.button = React.createRef();
    return {};
  },

  handleClick: function() {
    console.log(this.button.current);
  },

  render: function() {
    return <button ref={this.button} onClick={this.handleClick} />;
  }
});
```

In this version, we create the ref with the `React.createRef()` method. We have to call it when the `<App>` component is created, and before it's mounted to the DOM, so we have to do it inside the `getInitialState()` lifecycle method. Then we can pass the ref stored inside `this.button` into the `ref` prop of our `<button>` element.

The main difference in this example is the fact that we don't have to handle the update and storage of our element reference manually anymore, the ref object stored in `this.button` keeps track of all the renders for us. Also, we now have to use `this.button.current` to get the reference, and not `this.button`.

Wrap Up

In this chapter, we learned how to create refs. They are React's way to interact with DOM elements directly and only should be used as last resort when we can't implement a solution with `props` and `state` alone.

Two of the main reasons to use refs are:

- To keep track of focus in forms, when building these forms from scratch and no React based form library is used.

- To integrate third-party libraries that need direct DOM access.

In the **Advanced Integration** chapter, we talk about the last point in more detail.

Quiz

1. What are the two methods for creating a ref?
2. When is it appropriate to use a ref?
3. In what attribute of the ref-object is the actual ref stored?

Lesson 15 - Simple Integration

One of the most frequent tasks of software development is the integration of third-party libraries, and since the advent of the JavaScript package manager NPM, JavaScript projects have become well known for the accumulation of many small libraries.

In this chapter, we integrate a simple library, called Moment.js, into a React application. I've picked Moment.js because it's the most used Date library and it has a straightforward interface.

Including the Library

react-from-zero/15-simple-integration.html

```
<script src="https://unpkg.com/moment@2.18.1/min/moment.min.js">
```

First, we include the libraries source to our web-page. Because Moment.js is used all over the Web, there is a pre-built version ready to be loaded right in the browser with a <script> tag.

After the inclusion of the script, a global function moment() is available.

Using the Library

Now that the library is available on our website, we can use it from within a React component.

react-from-zero/15-simple-integration.html

```
var DateToday = function() {
  return <span>{moment().format("DD.MM.YYYY")}</span>;
};
```

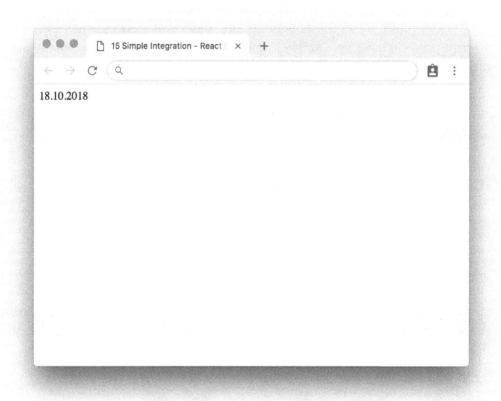

DateToday Component

We create a simple component that renders the current date. The call to moment() returns a Moment.js date-object that is pre-configured for the current date. The .format() method, called on the date-object, takes a template string it uses to format the date and returns a string where all the placeholders of the template string are replaced with real values.

JSX can render strings no problem, so we can now use the returned string, wrap it in a ‹span› element and return the whole thing.

We can use this ‹DateToday› component in our other components to display the current date everywhere in our React application.

Complex Example

We can also use objects created elsewhere and use them inside JSX.

Let's take this for example:

react-from-zero/15-simple-integration.html

```
var tomorrow = moment().add(1, "day");
```

The call to moment() returns a Moment.js date-object for the current day, the call to the .add() method lets us modify this date-object. We use it to add 1 day and get a date-object to store in the tomorrow variable.

While we can't use the object directly, we can use calls to its .format() method to extract formatted strings from it that can be used inside JSX' curly braces.

react-from-zero/15-simple-integration.html

```
var reactElement = (
  <div>
    <h1 style={{ textAlign: "center" }}>
      Tomorrow is {tomorrow.format("MMMM")} the{" "}
      {tomorrow.format("Do")}
    </h1>
    <DateToday />
  </div>
);
```

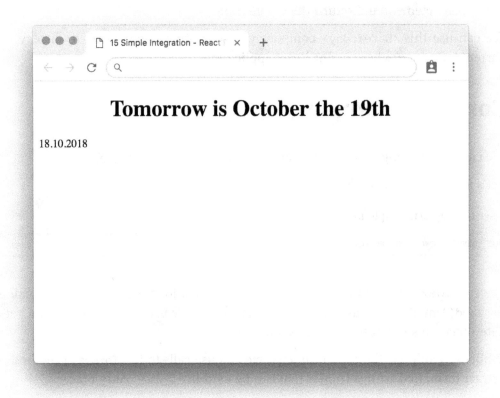

Object in JSX

Here we use it three times. Two times inside a sentence that tells us which day it is tomorrow, for example, "Tomorrow is January the 5th" and one time via our `<DateToday>` component from before.

Wrap Up

In this chapter, we learned how to integrate simple libraries into our React components.

While this is a straightforward example of a third party integration, it highlights the fact that React and JSX are **just** JavaScript that integrates with other JavaScript code flawlessly.

Quiz

1. How can JavaScript be called inside JSX?
2. Can third-party librarys be wrapped inside a component?
3. What data-types do third-party libraries have to return so we can use them directly in JSX?

Lesson 16 - Advanced Integration

In the last chapter, we talked about how to integrate simple libraries into React applications. The next step is to integrate more complex libraries.

Most libraries supply us with a bunch of functions that we can call and use their results, but sometimes some libraries need more to work. For example, map and chart libraries, which render graphics in some way often need direct access to a DOM element to do their work.

In this lesson, we'll use D3[12], a famous general data visualization library, together with React.

Including the Library

react-from-zero/16-advanced-integration.html

```
<script src="https://unpkg.com/d3@4.7.3/build/d3.min.js">
```

First, we include the libraries source to our web-page. D3, like Moment.js in the last lesson, is also a popular library, so there is a pre-built version ready to be loaded right in the browser with a `<script>` tag.

After the inclusion of the script, a global d3 object is available.

Using the Library

Like React, D3 needs access to a DOM element as a *root element* to render into.

Let's take this example:

---

[12]https://d3js.org/

```
d3.select("#app")
  .append("canvas")
  .node()
  .getContext("2d")
  .fillRect(10, 10, 100, 100);
```

In this example, we draw a black rectangle.

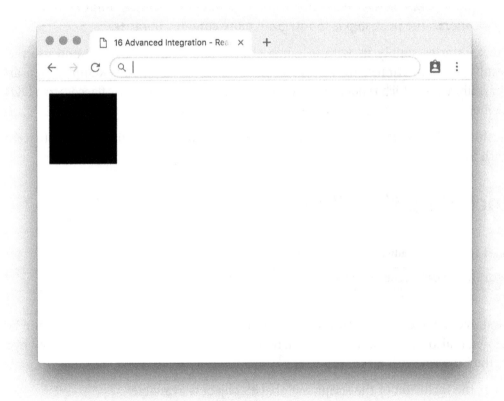

Black Rectangle

We use D3's select() method to get an object which holds a reference to the <div> element with the ID app. Then we use this object to append a <canvas> element to it. The node() method gets us a direct reference to the <canvas> so we can use it to get access to its drawing context, which we use to draw the rectangle.

The crux of this example is, we need the drawing context, and we can only obtain it from a <canvas> element, which is rendered somewhere in the DOM. React wants us to work with virtual DOM elements, which won't help us much here, so we need to resort to other methods of DOM interaction here.

Refs and Lifecycle Methods

We learned in previous lessons that React has some advanced features that kind of work as an escape hatch from the whole **unidirectional-dataflow** paradigm.

- Refs allow us to mark a virtual DOM element in JSX to tell React that we require a reference to it when it's rendered.
- The componentDidMount() lifecycle method allows us to do things when React rendered a virtual DOM element to the real DOM.

We can use these two features in tandem to tell React to render a <canvas> element, which we need for D3 and to notify us when it is available in the DOM.

```
var Square = createReactClass({
  getInitialState: function() {
    this.canvas = React.createRef();
    return {};
  },
  render: function() {
    return <canvas ref={this.canvas} />;
  },
  componentDidMount: function() {
    d3.select(this.canvas.current)
      .node()
      .getContext("2d")
      .fillRect(10, 10, 100, 100);
  }
});
```

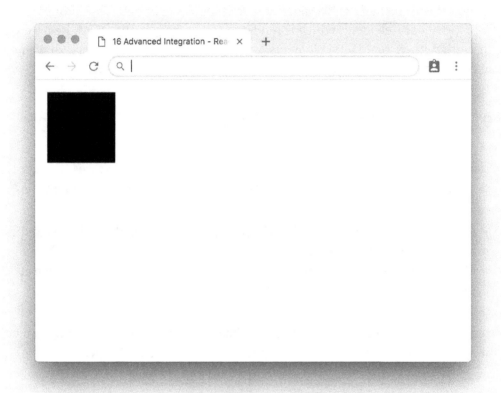

Square Component

1. The getInitialState() method is called, it creates a ref-object and stores it in this.canvas.
2. React calls the render() method, it tells React to render a <canvas> element and passes the ref-object created before to its ref prop.
3. When React rendered the <Square> component, and with it the <canvas> element, into the DOM it calls the componentDidMount() lifecycle method. In this method, the ref-object stored in this.canvas is now up-to-date, and it's current attribute holds a reference to the <canvas> element in the **real DOM**.
4. We can use this.canvas.current with D3's select() method to get the drawing context we need to draw the square.

Complex Example

We found out that the main problem of integrating some complex libraries is their need for direct DOM access. This can be a multitude of different things, like specific element or context types.

For more complex integrations, we can move the library interactions into a separate function and pass DOM references to it as arguments, when React finished doing its things.

Let's take this function:

react-from-zero/16-advanced-integration.html

```
function drawGraph(canvas, strokeColor) {
  // An example from
  // http://bl.ocks.org/mbostock/1b64ec067fcfc51e7471d944f51f1611
  // its released under the GPL-V3

  var n = 20;

  var nodes = d3.range(n * n).map(function(i) {
    return { index: i };
  });

  var links = [];

  for (var y = 0; y < n; ++y) {
    for (var x = 0; x < n; ++x) {
      if (y > 0)
        links.push({ source: (y - 1) * n + x, target: y * n + x });
      if (x > 0)
        links.push({ source: y * n + (x - 1), target: y * n + x });
    }
  }

  d3.forceSimulation(nodes)
```

```
    .force("charge", d3.forceManyBody().strength(-30))
    .force(
      "link",
      d3
        .forceLink(links)
        .distance(20)
        .iterations(10)
    )
    .on("tick", ticked);

var context = canvas.getContext("2d");
var width = canvas.width;
var height = canvas.height;

function ticked() {
  context.clearRect(0, 0, width, height);
  context.save();
  context.translate(width / 2, height / 2);

  context.beginPath();
  links.forEach(drawLink);
  context.strokeStyle = "#aaa";
  context.stroke();

  context.beginPath();
  nodes.forEach(drawNode);
  context.fill();
  context.strokeStyle = strokeColor;
  context.stroke();

  context.restore();
}

function drawLink(d) {
  context.moveTo(d.source.x, d.source.y);
  context.lineTo(d.target.x, d.target.y);
```

```
  }

  function drawNode(d) {
    context.moveTo(d.x + 3, d.y);
    context.arc(d.x, d.y, 3, 0, 2 * Math.PI);
  }
}
```

The drawGraph() function encapsulates all the D3 interactions. Its arguments are only a reference to a ‹canvas› element and a color configuration.

It does many things that seem quite complicated, but it does these only with the arguments supplied to it, and we know how to create these arguments before calling the function.

We can call this function in our React component from before with minimal changes.

```
var Visual = createReactClass({
  getInitalState: function() {
    this.canvas = React.createRef();
    return {};
  },
  render: function() {
    return <canvas ref={this.canvas} />;
  },
  componentDidMount: function() {
    drawGraph(this.canvas.current, this.props.color);
  }
});
```

- We have to rename the component to Visual.
- Then we use the drawGraph() function inside the componentDidMount() method, so we have the reference to the ‹canvas› element ready.
- As the second argument to the drawGraph() function, we pass the color prop of our Visual component.

Now we can use the Visual component like every other component in JSX even though it requires a third party library **and** direct DOM access to do its work and we didn't even use global DOM IDs for this, so if we create multiple copies of the component, they all work independently of each other.

react-from-zero/16-advanced-integration.html

```
var reactElement = (
  <div>
    <Visual color="#f00" />
    <Visual color="#0f0" />
    <Visual color="#00f" />
  </div>
);
```

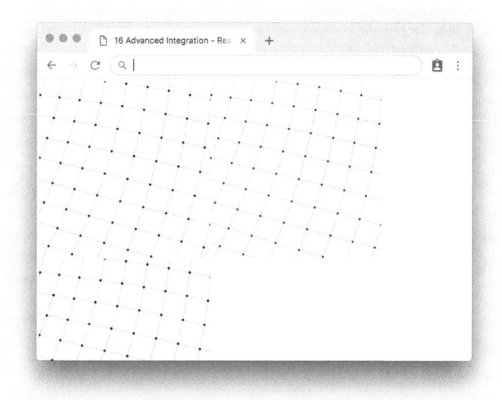

Fancy Graph

Wrap Up

In this lesson, we learned about a more complex approach to third-party integration.

- How to use refs to get direct access to the DOM
- How to use lifecycle methods to wait for the right moments for DOM access
- How refs are better than DOM IDs

Quiz

1. How do we get direct access to the DOM without a global ID?

2. In which lifecycle method can we access our DOM element the first time?
3. Which lifecycle method can we use to let our third-party library update the DOM element?

Lesson 17 - Unit Testing

Up until this point we've used a browser to run all of our examples. But for unit tests, we're going to take a different approach and use the command-line.

While there are solutions to run unit-tests in the browser too, the preferred way to do so for React applications is **a command-line tool called Jest**. It lets us test React components, how they render and the interaction with them.

It is possible to run parts of Jest inside the browser when switching to a test-runner line Mocha. With this setup, only rendering of components can be tested, but not the interaction with them.

Node Installation

While Jest is easy to set up, it needs to run in Node.js. So first, we need to install Node.js. We use the long-term-support version (LTS) 10 because it won't change too much in the next years.

The download is available via https://nodejs.org/, and the latest 10 version is okay.

Creating a Node.js Project

To create a new Node.js project, we need to create an empty directory and run `npm init` inside of it. This command will ask a few questions; the answers will be included in the `package.json` it creates.

For `test command:` we enter `jest`, because it's the tool we want to use later. It won't be installed yet, but at least the script that will call it later will be correct.

For the rest, use the default answers (mostly empty).

Installing Jest

Install Jest with: `npm install jest --save-dev`

This command changes the `package.json` by adding a new entry for Jest inside `devDependencies`. It also creates a lock-file, a `node_modules` directory, and download Jest and all of Jest's dependencies into this new directory.

We can now run Jest with: `npm test`

It displays `No tests found`, but that is okay.

Writing the First Test

To write our first test, we need to create a test file. Jest looks inside all directories, besides `node_modules` for files called `*.test.js` and try to run the tests inside them.

So let's create a `react.test.js` and write a simple test in it.

```
describe("Test", function() {
  it("runs", function() {
    expect(true).toBe(true);
  });
});
```

The `describe()` function takes a description and a callback. The callback will be filled with calls to the `it()` function, which also takes a description and a callback.

We can run the test with `npm test` and would see an output like this:

PASS ./react.test.js Test ☒ runs (5ms)

React Test Setup

Jest is now set up for basic testing, but we need some additional package to test our React components.

First, we need to include React. Previously we used React via CDN in a `<script>` tag, but now needs to be installed via NPM, like Jest.

Second, we need the `react-test-renderer` package. Which will have the effect of creating a "DOM" while we're running in Node.js.

We also have to **install the Babel compiler**, because we want to use JSX.

All can be installed with: `npm install react babel-jest babel-preset-env babel-preset-react react-test-renderer --save-dev`

Babel is pre-configured right when running in the Browser, but **we need to add a configuration file** when running it via Jest.

The file has to be named `.babelrc` and has to have the following content:

```
{
  "presets": ["env", "react"]
}
```

A call of `npm test` should now run without any errors.

 Another convenient way to setup a new React project with Jest is create-react-app[13]. While it is a *typical* way to create a React app, it also includes a lot of other features - so setting up `create-react-app` is beyond the scope of this book.

Testing React Components

After we have Jest up and running, we can finally start testing our React components.

Testing the Structure of a Component

Let's start with a simple component inside a file called `MyComponent.js`.

---

[13]https://reactjs.org/docs/create-a-new-react-app.html

```
var React = require("react");
function MyComponent(props) {
  return <span>Hello, World!</span>;
}
module.exports = MyComponent;
```

First we need to require React, because JSX makes calls to the React.createElement() function.

Then we define a simple component and export it, so a MyComponent.test.js file can require it.

The test file needs to look as follows:

```
var React = require("react");
var renderer = require("react-test-renderer");
var MyComponent = require("./MyComponent.js");

describe("MyComponent", function() {
  it("renders hello world", function() {
    var result = renderer.create(<MyComponent />).toJSON();
    expect(result.children[0]).toBe("Hello, World!");
  });
});
```

Because we use JSX in our test definition, we need to require React here too.

The test renderer is needed instead of React-DOM because no DOM is available in Node.js.

Finally, we need the component we want to test since we exported it in MyComponent.js, we can now require it in our test file.

In the test, we use the test renderer to get a JSON representation of our component. First, we call the create() method to enter the JSX we want to render, then we call the toJSON() to get a JavaScript object we can check.

Jest gives us a global expect() function we can use to test for different outcomes.

If we logged the `result` object, we would find out that it looks rather similar to the objects we encountered in lesson 0. It has `type`, `props` and `children`.

The only check our test performs is to look inside the `children` of our `result` object and expect it to be `"Hello, World!"`.

If we rerun Jest with `npm test` the result should look something like this:

PASS ./MyComponent.test.js MyComponent ☒ renders hello world (13ms)

This way we can ensure the structure of our rendered component.

Testing Interaction with a Component

Testing the structural integrity of our components is only one of the ways we can test components. We also want to test if *interactions* with our components work.

To do this, we need to test if event-handlers we pass into the `props` of our components get called at the right moments.

Jest offers a global method called `fn()` for this. It creates a function that keeps track of many things, like how often it was called.

So let's create a component with simple an interaction inside a new file called `MyButton.js`

```
var React = require("react");
function MyButton(props) {
  return <button onClick={props.onButtonPress}>Click Me!</button>;
}
module.exports = MyButton;
```

The component only wraps a `<button>` element and passes its `onButtonPress` prop into the buttons `onClick` prop.

Now we need a test for it, let's write it inside the `MyButton.test.js`

```
var React = require("react");
var renderer = require("react-test-renderer");
var MyButton = require("./MyButton.js");

describe("MyButton", function() {
  it("calls function on click", function() {
    var callback = jest.fn();
    var result = renderer
      .create(<MyButton onButtonPress={callback} />)
      .toJSON();
    result.props.onClick();
    expect(callback.mock.calls.length).toBe(1);
  });
});
```

This time we don't check the structure, we check how often the callback was called. We pass it into the onButtonPress prop of our component and then render everything with the help of the test renderer.

The result should have the callback we passed inside the onClick prop of the rendered <button> element; we created inside our MyButton component.

We call onClick once and check if the callback's calls.length is 1 now.

When we run Jest with npm test the output should look like this:

PASS ./MyButton.test.js MyButton ☒ calls function on click (13ms)

Wrap Up

In this chapter, we learned to setup React and Jest to run unit test inside the command-line.

We learned how to check the structure of and the interaction with our components.

Getting unit testing running for React is a bit more cumbersome than most of the things we learned in this book. It requires more than a browser and an Internet connection.

On the other hand, it can run everywhere a CLI tool can run, which makes things like continuous integration easier later.

Quiz

1. What kind of software is the Jest testing framework?
2. Which package do we need if we want to run React without a DOM?
3. How do we check if our callbacks got used correctly?

Lesson 18 - ES215

ECMAScript is the name of the specification of JavaScript. When new language features are added to JavaScript, they usually come from proposals to this specification.

In June 2015 the 6th version of ECMAScript was released, called ECMAScript 2015 or short ES2015.

When the 6th version was released, it was the most significant change to the language ever. It added new syntax for:

- classes
- functions
- block scoped and immutable variable declarations
- promises
- and much more.

Since React wanted to be future proof and these changes were effectively standardized and soon to be readily available in all major browsers, the React team decided to incorporate them into the React code-base and emphasize their use in their docs.

While I think this is the right approach, this led to a few problems for people who wanted to start with React – especially when they only know the previous versions of JavaScript.

People now had to learn React, JSX, and the new ES2015 concepts, not to speak of the whole tooling used to build and ship a React application. This often leads to students being overwhelmed or thinking some new language features are required or even part of React.

In **React From Zero** we've tried to teach React and JSX concepts **without needing to learn ES2015**. While this should bring people a solid understanding of how React works, **it does bring other problems**.

Because the default way to use React is with ES2015, production code-bases can confuse people who learned React without ES2015.

So in this lesson, I show you how the ES5 examples you learned can be mapped to the ES2015 code you will encounter at work.

Block Scope Variables

Let's start with the basics. There are two new ways to declare variables: `let` and `const`.

```
var a = 1; // "old" way
let b = 2;
const c = 3;
```

They both have block scope rather than function scope. This means if you declare a variable with `let` or `const` in a code-block these variables will only be visible inside this block. A code-block is some part of the code that is enclosed in curly braces {}, like used with `if`, `for`, `while`, `switch`.

Also, `const` variables can't be changed after their first assignment and have to be assigned a value at declaration time.

This is not React specific, but it since `let` and `const` behave differently than `var` it can lead to confusion.

Destructuring

One very heavily used feature, especially when working with `props` and `state` in React, is **destructuring**. It allows us to extract values as new variables from existing ones.

When used directly on function arguments, it often gets rid of extra variables.

It works with objects and arrays.

Destructuring an argument can happen directly inside the parenthesis of the function.

```
function MyButton(props) {
  return (
    <button onClick={props.onButtonClick}>{props.children}</button>
  );
}
```

Since props is an object, we can use the object-destructuring syntax on it:

```
function MyButton({ children, onButtonClick }) {
  return <button onClick={onButtonClick}>{children}</button>;
}
```

Array destructuring works similar and even allows creating a new array with the remaining values, not changing the source array in any way.

```
function MyList({ items }) {
  var [firstItem, ...rest] = items;
  return (
    <ul>
      <li>
        <b>{firstItem}</b>
      </li>
      {rest.map(function(item, index) {
        return <li key={index}>{item}</li>;
      })}
    </ul>
  );
}
```

In React this feature is mainly used to extract values from props and state before rendering.

Arrow Functions

There is a new way to declare a function, the arrow function.

This *arrow syntax* is often used to define anonymous functions or callbacks to event-handler props in React.

```
<button
  onClick={function(e) {
    console.log(e);
  }}
>
  click me
</button>
```

becomes

```
<button onClick={e => console.log(e)}>click me</button>
```

The parenthesis around the arguments is optional when only one argument is used, and the curly braces around the body are optional too if the last expression should be returned. The longer form of the above example callback would be `(e) => {return console.log(e)}`.

Besides being often faster to type, these functions have another benefit, **they keep their context**, so no re-binding of `this` before using them. Which is especially handy for callbacks that are executed asynchronously sometime in the future.

Some people prefer only to use this type of syntax for consistency reasons, so it's not uncommon to find a **functional component** defined with it.

```
function MyButton(props) {
  return <button onClick={props.onButtonClick}>Click Me</button>;
}
```

becomes

```
const MyButton = props => (
  <button onClick={props.onButtonClick}>Click Me</button>
);
```

The destructuring example from above would look like this:

```
const MyList = ({ items }) => {
  const [firstItem, ...rest] = items;
  return (
    <ul>
      <li>
        <b>{firstItem}</b>
      </li>
      {rest.map((item, index) => (
        <li key={index}>{item}</li>
      ))}
    </ul>
  );
};
```

Classes

One of ES2015 additions that lead to a considerable change in React code-bases were classes. While there were many ways to define a class system on top of JavaScripts prototype-based system, with classes finally getting there own standardized syntax, all these ways now converged.

In this book, we always used the createReactClass() function to create class components, but with ES2015's class syntax, this function isn't needed anymore.

```
var MyComponent = createReactClass({
  render: function() {
    return <h1>{this.props.name}</h1>;
  }
});
```

becomes

```
class MyComponent extends React.Component {
  render() {
    return <h1>{this.props.name}</h1>;
  }
}
```

Multiple things are happening in the new version.

First, it uses the new `class` syntax. While the inheritance was handled by the `createReactClass()` function before, we now have to extend `React.Component` manually.

React tries to keep inheritance to a minimum.

We only extend the React base-classes `React.Component` and `React.PureComponent` into concrete components we use in our app. We never create own base components we extend all our components from later.

The example also uses the **method shorthand** syntax. `{method: function() {}}` can now be written as `{method() {}}` in object- and class-definitions.

Method Binding

The `createReactClass()` function binds our methods to the components instance; the ES2015 class syntax don't. All the methods called by React, like `render()` or the lifecycle methods, have the right `this`, but our methods which we may create for event handlers don't.

Let's look at the following example:

```
class MyComponent extends React.Component {
  constructor() {
    super();
    this.value = 10;
  }

  handleClick(e) {
    console.log(this.value);
  }

  render() {
    return <button onClick={this.handleClick}>Click me!</button>;
  }
}
```

This example uses the constructor() method to initialize an instance attribute value.

 The super() function has to be called before accessing this in a constructor of an extending class. Since we extend React.Component we need to call it, or else we get an error.

Later we try to access this.value in our event handler method handleClick(). This would result in an undefined logging, because this can be anything. The **method shorthand** syntax is just a shorthand for function() {} and not for () => {} and we learned that only the new arrow syntax binds this correctly.

 The this keyword is a tricky thing in JavaScript because non-arrow-functions don't bind themselfs to the this of the place they're defined, but to the this of the place they're executed. This is also true for methods. If we pass a method as an event-handler to an element;this isn't our component anymore at the time the click is triggered and so we don't have access to the components attributes.

To fix this, we can either wrap the method with an arrow function in the render() method or bind it manually in the constructor.

```
// ...
render() {
  return <button onClick={e => this.handleClick(e)}>Click me!</button>;
}
// ...
```

The arrow function is bound to the `this` of the `render()` method, so it's available when the event triggers too.

```
// ...
constructor() {
  super();
  this.value = 10;
  this.handleClick = this.handleClick.bind(this);
}
// ...
```

The classic way is to bind manually. We can be safe that the `this` in the constructor is the right one, so we can bin to it here and replace our method with a correctly bound version of itself.

Modules

The next significant addition is modules. They are often called ES-modules, because, like with classes, JavaScript developers already created their systems and this is an attempt to standardize all of them to improve integration.

React project started to integrate this system early on, so you certainly will encounter it in your projects.

Exporting and Importing

The first principle of this modules system is, by default all values are private to the file, so you don't can create global variables by accident. If you need a global variable, you have to attach it explicitly to the global `window` object.

If we want to use a value outside of a file, we need to export it. In the context of React, this is significant, since most custom components map directly to one file.

There are two ways to export. We can export default ..., which is often used for the main export of the file. We can also export ..., which leads to a named export, which allows for multiple exports in one file.

In other files, we can then import these exported values, depending on how they were exported.

If the variable was exported as default we could choose our name freely in the importing file.

If the variable was exported with a name, we have to use that name in the importing file.

Here some examples:

```
// MyComponent.js
function MyComponent() {
  return <h1>Hello</h1>;
}
export default MyComponent;
```

```
// x.js
import MyComponent from "./MyComponent.js";
```

```
// MyComponent.js
export default function MyComponent() {
  return <h1>Hello</h1>;
}
```

```
// x.js
import MyComponent from "./MyComponent.js";
```

```
// MyComponent.js
export function MyComponent() {
  return <h1>Hello</h1>;
}
```

```
// x.js
import { MyComponent } from "./MyComponent.js";
```

```
// constants.js
export const MY_CONSTANT = 10;
```

```
// x.js
import { MY_CONSTANT } from "./constants.js";
```

```
// values.js
export {
  valueA: 10,
  valueB: 20
}
```

```
// x.js
import {valueA, valueB} from "./values.js";
```

Wrap Up

In this lesson, we learned about the main differences between using React with ES5 and ES2015.

- Block scope variable declarations with let and const
- Destructuring objects and arrays
- Short function definition with =>
- Standardized class definition with the class

- Standardized module definition with `export` and `import`

While there were many new additions with ES2016, ES2017 and so on, these are the most important ones when working with React.

Quiz

1. Can we use ES5 and ES2015 features together in one code-base?
2. What problem does the arrow (=>) function definition solve?
3. How do callback methods behave differently when using `class` instead of the `createReactClass()` function?

Virtual DOM Primer

Remember that the Virtual DOM lets us write our code as if we overwrite our DOM nodes, while still getting good performance.

The **virtual DOM** (VDOM), is just a fancy name for **plain old JavaScript objects** nested to resemble the structure of a DOM.

React then takes this VDOM, runs a diff algorithm with the previous version and calculates the minimum of changes that are needed to make the DOM look like the new VDOM.

This approach allows you to focus on your data and UI and frees you from meddling with the details of DOM updates - all while getting super-fast performance.

A simple virtual DOM implementation

The spirit of this tutorial is to **demystify the magic behind React**. To that end, let's write a simple VDOM implementation.

This version will just mimic the most fundamental React function (and wont do any "diffing", a speed optimization), but **it helps to understand what is happening** when you tell React to *render* your app.

Lets say our VDOM looks like this:

simple-vdom/index.html

```
var simpleVDom = {
  type: "p",
  props: {},
  children: ["Hello, World!"]
};
```

It has a type, props and children. The type tells us it's a paragraph, and it has one child, some text that says "Hello, world!" and no props. This gets sent into the next part, the render function, as the vDom parameter.

simple-vdom/index.html

```
function render(target, vDom) {
  var domRootElement = document.getElementById(target);

  domRootElement.innerHTML = "";
  domRootElement.appendChild(createDomElement(vDom));
}
```

This function gets the target (real) *DOM* element that the (virtual) *VDOM* should be rendered into and clears its content.

Next, it **creates real DOM elements** from the VDOM with the help of createDomElement, and appends it to **the target DOM element**.

The createDomElement is where the magic happens. It:

- traverses the VDOM
- creates real DOM elements, with attributes and event handlers
- links them together and returns one element which
- gets appended to the target element in render function.

Let's go through it, step by step. Because this is a recursive function, we need to know if we've reached a "leaf" node. Meaning, in this case, that we've reached some inner text:

simple-vdom/index.html

```
function createDomElement(vDomElement) {
  if (typeof vDomElement == "string")
    return document.createTextNode(vDomElement);
```

Above, we check if the element is a string. If it is, then are at a leaf of the VDOM tree and we need to create a TextNode, with the string as its content. We'll return it and we have nothing else to do in this case.

Next, we know we have a non-text element, so we create one with the help of the type attribute of our VDOM object:

simple-vdom/index.html

```
21    var domElement = document.createElement(vDomElement.type);
```

In our implementation, like React, an element can now have HTML attributes and event handlers. For example, we might want an element that has a style tag or an element that responds to a click.

Remember that in React, we pass in this attributes through the props key. Here we iterate through props and:

- add an event handler if the propName starts with "on" (e.g. onClick)
- or add a "regular" attribute otherwise.

simple-vdom/index.html

```
22    for (var propName in vDomElement.props) {
23      if (propName.startsWith("on")) {
24        domElement.addEventListener(
25          propName.substring(2).toLowerCase(),
26          vDomElement.props[propName]
27        );
28      } else {
29        domElement.setAttribute(propName, vDomElement.props[propName]);
30      }
31    }
```

Lastly, we apply the createDomElement function recursively for every child that our current VDOM element has. If every child has been processed we return the freshly generated DOM tree:

simple-vdom/index.html

```
34    for (var i in vDomElement.children)
35      domElement.appendChild(createDomElement(vDomElement.children[i]));
36
37    return domElement;
38  }
```

Complete createDomElement

Here's what the completed createDomElement looks like all-together:

simple-vdom/index.html

```
17  function createDomElement(vDomElement) {
18    if (typeof vDomElement == "string")
19      return document.createTextNode(vDomElement);
20
21    var domElement = document.createElement(vDomElement.type);
22
23    for (var propName in vDomElement.props) {
24      if (propName.startsWith("on")) {
25        domElement.addEventListener(
26          propName.substring(2).toLowerCase(),
27          vDomElement.props[propName]
28        );
29      } else {
30        domElement.setAttribute(propName, vDomElement.props[propName]);
31      }
32    }
33
34    for (var i in vDomElement.children)
```

```
35        domElement.appendChild(createDomElement(vDomElement.children[i]));
36
37    return domElement;
38  }
```

A more complex element

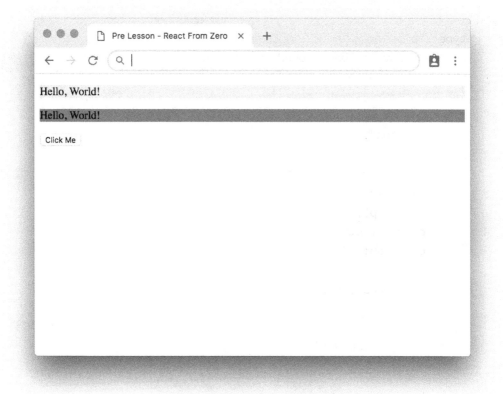

Complex element

A more complex VDOM could look like this:

simple-vdom/index.html

```
48  var vDom = {
49    type: "div",
50    props: { class: "container" },
51    children: [
52      {
53        type: "p",
54        props: { style: "background: yellow" },
55        children: ["Hello, World!"]
56      },
57      {
58        type: "p",
59        props: { style: "background: red" },
60        children: ["Hello, World!"]
61      },
62      {
63        type: "button",
64        props: {
65          onClick: function (event) {
66            vDom.children.push({
67              type: "p",
68              props: { style: "background: yellow" },
69              children: ["Added by a click!"]
70            });
71            render("app", vDom);
72          }
73        },
74        children: ["Click Me"]
75      }
76    ]
77  };
```

As you can see in this example, there are many children and even some props, some of which you probably know from HTML. We have a division with a container CSS class, some paragraphs with CSS styles and text and a button that has an onClick handler and text. The handler of the button adds a paragraph to the VDOM and calls the render function again with it.

Conclusion

This is a very basic implementation of VDOM rendering, it breaks down in many cases and doesn't have the diffing algorithms that calculate the minimal changes needed that made React famous.

The point I want to make here is that this simple implementation has almost the same interface as React's render function.

You give it a VDOM element, with children and props and it will render it for you into the DOM as fast as it can.

So going on to the next chapters, you can use this as a mental model for what's happening behind the scenes.

Changelog

Revision 3 - 2018-10-28

- Added Chapter 14, *Integration with JavaScript Libraries*
- Added Chapter 15, *Advanced Integration with D3*
- Added Chapter 16, *Unit Testing*
- Added Chpater 17, *ES2015*
- Added quizzes to all chapters

Revision 2 - 2018-10-17

- Rewrite Chapter 10 - Pomodoro Timer App
- Added Chapter 11, *Lifecycle Methods*
- Added Chapter 12, *Component Refactor*
- Added Chapter 13, *References*

Revision 1 - 2018-09-28

First pre-release edition.